MOVING MOUNTAINS

Praying with Passion,
Confidence, and Authority

JOHN ELDREDGE

NELSON
BOOKS

An Imprint of Thomas Nelson

Published in Nashville, Tennessee, by Nelson Books, an imprint of Thomas Nelson. Nelson Books and Thomas Nelson are registered trademarks of HarperCollins Christian Publishing, Inc.

Published in association with Yates & Yates, www.yates2.com.

Thomas Nelson titles may be purchased in bulk for educational, business, fund-raising, or sales promotional use. For information, please e-mail SpecialMarkets@ThomasNelson.com.

Any Internet addresses, phone numbers, or company or product information printed in this book are offered as a resource and are not intended in any way to be or to imply an endorsement by Thomas Nelson, nor does Thomas Nelson vouch for the existence, content, or services of these sites, phone numbers, companies, or products beyond the life of this book.

Unless otherwise noted, Scripture quotations are taken from the Holy Bible, New International Version®, NIV®. Copyright © 1973, 1978, 1984 by Biblica, Inc.™ Used by permission of Zondervan. All rights reserved worldwide. www.zondervan.com

Scripture quotations marked UPDATED NIV are taken from the HOLY BIBLE, NEW INTERNATIONAL VERSION®, NIV® Copyright © 1973, 1978, 1984, 2011 by Biblica, Inc.® Used by permission. All rights reserved worldwide.

Scripture quotations marked NLT are taken from the *Holy Bible*, New Living Translation. © 1996. Used by permission of Tyndale House Publishers, Inc., Wheaton, Illinois 60189. All rights reserved.

Scripture quotations marked MSG are taken from *The Message* by Eugene H. Peterson. © 1993, 1994, 1995, 1996, 2000. Used by permission of NavPress Publishing Group. All rights reserved.

Scripture quotations marked NASB are taken from the NEW AMERICAN STANDARD BIBLE®. © The Lockman Foundation 1960, 1962, 1963, 1968, 1971, 1972, 1973, 1975, 1977, 1995. Used by permission.

Scripture quotations marked NKJV are taken from THE NEW KING JAMES VERSION. © 1982 by Thomas Nelson, Inc. Used by permission. All rights reserved.

Scripture quotations marked KJV are taken from the KING JAMES VERSION. Public domain.

ISBN: 978-0-7180-8859-0 (TP)
ISBN: 978-0-7180-7953-6 (IE)
ISBN: 978-0-7180-3766-6 (e-book)

Library of Congress Cataloging-in-Publication Data

Names: Eldredge, John, 1960-
Title: Moving mountains : praying with passion, confidence, and authority / John Eldredge.
Description: Nashville : Thomas Nelson, 2016. | Includes bibliographical references.
Identifiers: LCCN 2015027220 | ISBN 9780718037512
Subjects: LCSH: Prayer--Christianity.
Classification: LCC BV210.3 .E43 2016 | DDC 248.3/2--dc23 LC record available at http://lccn.loc.gov/2015027220

Printed in the United States of America

17 18 19 20 21 RRD 6 5 4 3 2 1

To the men and women who taught me to pray—I am forever changed.

CONTENTS

CONTENTS

One

PRAYER THAT WORKS

June 26, 2012, was a simmering summer day in Colorado. Thermometers in Colorado Springs would report a record-breaking high of 101°F—fueling concerns about a wildfire burning unchecked in the mountains west of town. Fire crews were spread thin, and drought conditions had prepped the hillsides like tinder. Many worried eyes were turned toward the hills that day. Then, as if on some malevolent cue, winds started gusting to sixty-five miles an hour. (A thirty-five-mile-per-hour blast will almost knock you over, to give you some perspective; sixty-five miles per hour is considered a "violent storm" on the Beaufort Wind Scale.) Storm winds and flames on dry mountain terrain make for an unholy trinity.

The Waldo Canyon Fire jumped containment lines. Like the German blitzkrieg racing across Poland in 1939, it began sweeping east toward the city limits, unchecked and ravening. When all was said and done, 18,247 acres and 346 homes were consumed.

I was sitting at my desk that afternoon when a colleague walked in and said, "Have you seen this?" My instinctive reaction was to look to the mountains—our office windows face west—and I saw the vanguard of the fire cresting the last ridge before town. We'd been following the reports hour to hour; the fire had grown to 4,000 acres and was deemed only 5 percent contained. My neighborhood (we border the forest) had been placed on evacuation warning twice, and for days we watched the column of smoke rising over the mountains from the fire's epicenter west of us, billowing to a height of thirty thousand feet like a thunderhead or the plume of a volcano, all orange and black and foreboding.

But the reports kept assuring us that the fire would move north and west and bypass town, so we went on with our lives—until I saw the advancing flames crest the ridge. I grabbed my phone as I walked out the door and called Stasi. "Pack up; I'm headed home." "They haven't given the evacuation notice," she said. "It's coming," I told her. "The fire is coming. I can see it. I'm on my way." Like a man running before an incoming tide, I literally raced the fire home as it swept ridge after ridge. We grabbed the dog and a few belongings—it's true, what they say, how little actually matters to you when it comes down to "the moment"—and said good-bye to everything else.

Our neighbors were the last to leave; they later told us that trees on the hill above our houses were exploding. Stuck in the traffic jams caused by the evacuation, ashes drifting down like snowflakes, we frantically called and texted friends asking for prayer. My '78 Land Cruiser has no air conditioning, so I soaked a scarf of Stasi's in water and held it to my mouth to prevent smoke inhalation while I made contingency plans should the fire catch up to us; the winds were howling down the mountain now, driving the flames forward like the hounds of hell.

We took cover east of town with some dear friends and watched anxiously. It would be three more days of fire and smoke and shrouded hillsides till we heard the news—our home had been spared.

Bits and pieces of story began to trickle in, but it was the reports of the fire crews that left us speechless. A veteran fire chief and a handful of wildfire "hot shots" had gathered on our street to stand in wonder as they witnessed something they had never seen before. The one-hundred-foot wall of flame should have swept down our summer-crisp hillside and engulfed our home in a matter of seconds. But it did not. Every time the advancing fury approached our property line, it wavered, hesitated, and pulled back. The raging furnace would not cross our property line. It would advance, then retreat, advance, then retreat—though the winds were at its back and the fire had just covered miles in a manner of minutes. We realized it was at that same moment, three days earlier, that a friend had texted us,

I saw an angel, above your house, spreading its wings and flapping them against the wind and the fire. I think you are going to be okay.

When we finally were allowed back into the neighborhood, we found that the low-lying grass fire had burned right up to our porch. But the major assault had not crossed our property line. The aspen trees in our yard were still in their summer glory.

I know, I know—the story raises some difficulties; it touches the raw nerve of your own longing for rescue and your history

3

of unanswered prayers. Other people were earnestly praying as the fire swept down—how come their homes weren't spared? I don't pretend to know the answer to that. Like you, I have my own story of prayers answered, prayers unanswered, and silence I can't quite make sense of. This is not a story about my prayers at all. What I do know is this: every day, when I step out my door, I see up on the hill the outline of blackened tree stumps, and then, coming closer, after you cross our property line, green, living trees. One side looks like Mordor, the other, Eden. An irrefutable witness to the power of prayer.

A Disruptive But Hopeful Truth

Look, let's go ahead and name the elephant in the room—some prayers work, and some prayers don't. Why does that surprise and irritate us? Some diets work, but most don't; no one is really surprised by that. We simply keep looking for the one that will work for us. Some investments produce, and others don't; you look for the program that works for you. Some schools are effective while others fail badly; hopefully you can find the situation that is right for your child. *There is a way things work.* Can you name anything in life where this isn't so?

I damaged my elbow last summer doing some yard work. I ignored the problem for weeks until I was forced to see my physical therapist. I went under the assumption that a couple visits ought to take care of my problem; after all, it was just a strain— it's not like I broke it or something. Yet therapy took *months*, and I was so irritated by that. And it was irritated at me; that is, I kept irritating the muscle by using my elbow before it was healed. I

4

kept aggravating it because I didn't want to accommodate my life-style to account for the realities of a tiny muscle in my left elbow.

You know the irritation I speak of. Something adolescent in human nature just doesn't like having to submit to the realities of the world around us (and within us). We want to eat whatever we feel like eating; then we are surprised and dismayed when our health collapses down the road. We want exercise or weight loss to come quickly and easily; we want it to fit neatly into our calendar. We want our friends to be good to us, without ever having to look at how our personalities impact them. We want our kids to "turn out" without making the sacrifices in our parenting styles that are required to fit their needs.

And so it is with prayer. We just want it to be simple and easy; we want it to go like this:

God is loving and powerful.
We need his help.
So we ask for help, as best we know how.
The rest is up to him.
After all—he's God. He can do anything.

The problem is, sometimes he comes through, often he doesn't, and we have no idea for the rhyme or reason why. We lose heart and abandon prayer. (And we feel hurt and justified in doing so.) We abandon the very treasure God has given us for *not* losing heart, for moving the "mountains" in front of us, bringing about the changes we so desperately want to see in our world.

The uncomfortable truth is this: *that is a very naïve view of prayer*, on a level with believing that all a marriage needs is love, or that we should base our foreign policy on belief in our fellow man.

That simple view of prayer has crushed many a dear soul, because it ignores crucial facts. There is a way things work.

God is powerful, I ask for help, and now it's up to him—it reminds me of a scene from the movie *Patch Adams*. Patch is a young medical student with a heart of gold; he wants to offer health care to the disenfranchised. He rallies a group of like-minded idealists, and they begin to chase their dreams. Then tragedy strikes; Patch's girlfriend is murdered by a schizophrenic man who was among the outcasts they were trying to rescue. The scene then takes us to a cliff top; Patch is standing on the brink. The mood is ominous; it appears he is about to take his life. Patch is arguing with God. I like that part very much—he is reaching out; he is wrestling in the right place. Then he reveals his misunderstanding of the world:

> [Patch is looking up to heaven]
>
> "Answer me please—tell me what you're doing."
>
> [Silence.]
>
> "Okay, let's look at the logic: You create man. Man suffers enormous amounts of pain. Man dies. Maybe you should have had just a few more brainstorming sessions prior to creation."
>
> [A pause]
>
> "You rested on the seventh day; maybe you should have spent that day on compassion."[1]

His understanding is incomplete—*dangerously* incomplete. It leaves out some awfully essential facts from that story:

> "You create man. Man chooses to rebel against you. We hand our lives, the earth, and the history of the human race over

to the evil one. All our misery flows from this fact. But you
intervene—you sent your Son to redeem us, and restore us.
Now we find ourselves in an epic war for the human race and
the planet."

Do you see what a difference those "omissions" make?! You
cannot begin to understand something like murder or wildfire
without those elements of the story. Nor can you understand why
some prayers work while others don't.

There Are Answers

Prayer sets up a terrible dilemma for us. We want to pray; it's in
our nature. We desperately want to believe that God will come
through for us. But then . . . he doesn't seem to, and where does
that leave us?

 I believe God is in the dilemma; I believe he wants us to push
through to real answers, solid answers.

For one thing, this reality we find ourselves in is *far* more
dynamic than most folks have been led to believe—especially
people of faith. Like Patch, we hold dangerously incomplete
understandings of our situation, such as,

God is all-powerful.
He did not intervene.
So it must not be his will to intervene.

Yes—God is sovereign. And in his sovereignty he created a
world in which the choices of men and angels matter. Tremendously.

He has granted to us "the dignity of causation," as Pascal called it. Our choices have enormous consequences. We will have much more to say about this going forward, but prayer is *not* as simple as, "I asked; God didn't come. I guess he doesn't want to."

We have embarked on the most exciting story possible, filled with danger, adventure, and wonders. There is nothing more hopeful than the thought that things can be different, we *can* move mountains, and we have some role in bringing that change about.

Maybe we can begin to find some answers, or at least a new way of looking at things, in a short story from the Old Testament. During the reign of King Ahab (circa 860 BC), the Middle East was leveled by a three-and-a-half-year drought. Crops failed; famine swept the land; herds of livestock were "put down" because there wasn't a wild tuft of grass to keep them alive. It was a scene right out of the twentieth-century American dust bowl, or the more recent famines in Africa. But relief was close at hand; God spoke to the prophet Elijah that the time of the drought had come to an end: "After a long time, in the third year, the word of the LORD came to Elijah: 'Go and present yourself to Ahab, and I will send rain on the land'" (1 Kings 18:1).

Finally, the heavens were going to relent; rain was coming; a real gully-washer was headed their way, a genuine biblical deluge—the kind that sinks ox carts up to their axles in mud and gives the kids a week off school. But before it could all happen— and this is the first fascinating wrinkle in the story—Elijah had to pray it would rain. Now, why is that? Why didn't God simply send the rain? We don't know; we have to stick with the story . . .

> Elijah climbed to the top of Carmel, bent down to the ground and put his face between his knees. "Go and look toward the

sea," he told his servant. And he went up and looked. "There is nothing there," he said. Seven times Elijah said, "Go back." The seventh time the servant reported, "A cloud as small as a man's hand is rising from the sea." So Elijah said, "Go and tell Ahab, 'Hitch up your chariot and go down before the rain stops you.'" Meanwhile, the sky grew black with clouds, the wind rose, a heavy rain came on and Ahab rode off to Jezreel. (vv. 42–45)

I love this narrative; it is so practical, and immensely helpful when it comes to understanding prayer and how it works. God is going to come through alright, but he insists on involving Elijah's prayers. It reminds me of Augustine's line, "Without God, we cannot, and without us, he will not." We find ourselves in the sort of universe where prayer plays a crucial role, sometimes, the deciding role. Our choices matter.

Next, Elijah doesn't just take a quick whack at it; no little "cut-flower" prayers here, as Eugene Peterson calls them. No little "Jesus, be with us today" prayers. Elijah is determined to see results. He bows, and prays, and then sends his manservant to see if it's working—is it having any effect? I love his posture, his willingness to give it a go, see what happens, and then adjust himself to the results. The servant comes back and reports that the sky is bleak and empty, just as it has been for years, barren as old Sarai's womb. This is the point at which most of us give up, but the old prophet sticks at it; he has another go and sends his man to have a second look. Nothing. So he takes his cloak off, puts his shoulder to the wheel, and gives it yet another try. He's not letting the evidence discourage him.

Six more times he sticks with it. By now the rest of us would have bailed down to Starbucks to commiserate about "the dark night of the soul," and what to do with "the silence of God." Not this old Israelite—he's still up on the mountain, persevering. After eight rounds of prayer—and *rounds* really does feel like the right word by this point; you get the feeling they are like rounds in the ring, full of sweat and grit and a real going at it—after the eighth bell the servant says, "Well . . . there's a puff of cloud on the horizon, not any bigger than your fist" and that's all it takes; the storm is on its way.

Contrast this with a story Anne Lamott shared in her auto-biographical book *Traveling Mercies*. She was recounting her somewhat justified paranoia over possible melanoma (her father died from melanoma) and a six-week wait to get a biopsy done. Anne had returned home from her dermatologist and was pray-ing: "So I wrote God a note on a scrap of paper. It said, 'I am a little anxious. Help me remember that you are with me even now. I am going to take my sticky fingers off the control panel until I hear from you.' Then I folded up the note and put it in the drawer of the table next to my bed as if it were God's In box."[2]

Now, I like Anne Lamott very much; I think it is a touching story, so true to our humanity. But it is just not helpful when it comes to prayer. Whose prayers do you think are more likely to see results—Elijah's or Lamott's? If you were going to ask one of the two of them to pray for someone you love, who would you choose?

So let's be honest—some prayers work, and some prayers don't. We might be embarrassed to admit that, but you know it's true. If you are interested in prayer at all, you are interested in prayer that works. *That* kind of prayer is the focus of this book. Which brings us back to Elijah the Tishbite. There is an over-looked passage late in the New Testament that is going to begin to connect some dots for us in a wild way. It comes from the book of James, and he brings us back around to the old man praying on the mountain: "The prayer of a righteous man is powerful and effective. Elijah was a man just like us. He prayed earnestly that it would not rain, and it did not rain on the land for three and a half years. Again he prayed, and the heavens gave rain, and the earth produced its crops" (5:16–18).

The brother of Jesus was giving his readers a tutorial on the subject of prayer. (He had seen some serious demonstrations of prayer, we might recall, growing up around the man who turned a boy's lunch into an all-you-can-eat buffet for five thousand.) James pointed to the famous drought story I just cited, then made a staggering connection—you are no different than Elijah. That was his purpose in using the phrase, "Elijah was a man just like us." James was trying to disarm that religious posture that so often poisons the value of biblical stories: *Well, sure, that was so-and-so* [in this case Elijah] *and they were different than us.* Nope. Not the case. Actually, James makes it very clear: Elijah was a human being just like you.

In other words, *you can do it too.*

I'm not going to try and convince you that you ought to pray. If the struggles of those you love, the heartache of the world, or your own dreams, desires, and afflictions do not move you, nothing I say here would be more compelling.

What I can do is put a far, far more effective understanding of prayer in your hands, together with enough applications that you begin to get a feel for how things work. There is a way things work. But first, let's lift off our hearts a few of those dangerous misunderstandings in the way we look at God and prayer.

Two

THIRD GRADERS
AT NORMANDY

I am among the millions who have fallen in love with the Chronicles of Narnia series. We shared them as a family when our boys were young, and we continue to love them as adults. (The books, by the way, are much, much better than the movies; if you've only met the stories in film, you must go back and read the originals!) In fact, Stasi and I are currently reading aloud book six, *The Silver Chair*, to each other in the evenings. I'm struck this time around by just how dangerous an adventure the children are tasked with. In chapter 2 they meet Aslan on his own mountain, and Jill is told why he has summoned them out of our world and into Narnia:

> And now hear your task. Far from here in the land of Narnia there lives an aged king who is sad because he has no prince of his blood to be king after him. He has no heir because his only son was stolen from him many years ago, and no one in Narnia

knows where that prince went or whether he is still alive. But he is. I lay on you this command, that you seek this lost prince until either you have found him and brought him to his father's house, or else died in the attempt, or else gone back into your own world.[1]

Wait—that second piece—*died in the attempt*?! My goodness. These are grave orders for a couple of ten-year-olds. Aslan is the best, kindest, most Jesus-like figure you'll ever meet in literature. *This* is the sort of story he has for them? Would you send your fifth grader off to Somalia? And yet, I think author C. S. Lewis was onto something very true about the character of God and the world in which we find ourselves.

The children are being called up.

We see a similar theme in J. R. R. Tolkien's *The Hobbit*. Gandalf arranges for young Bilbo Baggins to join a company of dwarves on their quest to recover the Lonely Mountain, and the treasure that lies buried in its halls. The young hobbit has never held a sword, never slept outdoors, never even been beyond the borders of the Shire. He loves books, teatime, and his armchair, and he always carries a handkerchief. Furthermore, Gandalf does not know for certain whether or not the dragon Smaug—"Chiefest and Greatest of all Calamities"—is lying there in dreadful malice.[2] Bilbo could be walking into a trap.

Now remember—Gandalf loves Bilbo, loves him dearly. Yet he is sending him on a very dangerous adventure from which he cannot promise the hobbit he will even return. Then he adds, "And if you do, you will not be the same . . ."[3]

Which brings me to the first of two assumptions essential to prayer:

God Is Growing Us All Up

I write to you, dear children,

> because your sins have been forgiven on account
> of his name.

I write to you, fathers,

> because you have known him who is from the
> beginning.

I write to you, young men,

> because you have overcome the evil one. (1 John
2:12–13)

Children, fathers, young men—how beautiful. How kind of John to remind us we are all at different places in our spiritual journeys. We are at different stages of *maturing*. "Children" in the faith know the basics—they know they are forgiven. The "young men" (and women) know other things—they understand the battle. "Fathers" (and mothers) are further along still—they know God intimately. We are all underway and we are *not* all in the same place; this is very gracious, and realistic, and quite helpful when it comes to understanding your own life or the lives of those around you. If you think about it, you can probably name the children, young men, and fathers (and mothers) in your life.

God understands where you are. As George MacDonald assured us, "What father is not pleased with the first tottering attempt of his little one to walk?"

And, God is absolutely committed to your growing up: "What father would be satisfied with anything but the manly step of the full-grown son or daughter?"[4]

Elijah was probably once like Lamott; Lamott is on her way to becoming an Elijah. To this, God has committed himself most fervently.

As it was for many parents before, teaching our sons to drive was a hair-raising endeavor—merging into traffic that felt like Han Solo pushing the Millennium Falcon into light speed; sudden braking that seemed equally certain to send me through the windshield. They were giving it a go; it was terrifying and I was so proud of them. I was delighted with their efforts. But of course, I would be more than disappointed if their driving was the same now, ten years later. So it is with God—he is utterly delighted with our attempts at prayer; he loves our little prayers tucked into drawers. And, he is calling us upward to grow into the maturity we were destined for, including mature prayers. Elijah was not tucking little prayers under rocks on the mountain. I doubt very much it would have rained if he had.

But here is the problem—most of us don't quite share God's fervent passion for our maturity. Really, now, if you stopped ten people at random on their way out of church next Sunday and polled them, I doubt very much that you would find one in ten who said, "Oh, my first and greatest commitment this afternoon is to mature!" Like Bilbo, our natural investments lie in other things—lunch, a nap, the game, our general comfort, including getting others to cooperate with our agendas.

Yet there is no mistaking the theme in Scripture: God is committed to growing us up:

> . . . until we all reach unity in the faith and in the knowledge of
> the Son of God and become mature . . . (Eph. 4:13)

. . . wrestling in prayer for you, that you may stand firm in all the will of God, mature and fully assured. (Col. 4:12)

Brothers, stop thinking like children. (1 Cor. 14:20)

Therefore let us leave the elementary teachings about Christ and go on to maturity, not laying again the foundation of repentance from acts that lead to death, and of faith in God, instruction about baptisms, the laying on of hands, the resurrection of the dead, and eternal judgment. (Heb. 6:1–2)

Wait—knowing how to heal the sick by the laying on of hands is considered first-grade–level stuff? I think I missed that class. But the call to grow up is very clear. And how does God provide for growing us up? What are his *means*? Situations that stretch us, strain us, push us beyond what we thought we could endure—those very same circumstances that cause us to pray.

This assumption is important for one simple reason: it changes your expectations. When you show up at the gym, you are not surprised or irritated that the trainer pushes you into a drenching sweat; it's what you came for. But you'd be furious if your housemate expected this of you when you flop home on the couch after a long day's work. (Perhaps you might begin to see the connection in some of your feelings toward God.)

Bilbo, Jill, and Eustace are being called up. And suddenly, they find themselves in dangerous parts of the world, facing threats they never dreamed of. Which brings me to the second assumption critical to effective prayer, a core assumption the Scripture holds about your life.

We Are at War

News reports in the fall of 2014 about the execution of children by ISIS guerrillas left us all speechless. We received a number of desperate e-mails crying out for prayer. Islamic extremists were going through villages in Iraq executing men, women, and children. Christian families were among those targeted (surely you read the reports). A family would be dragged from their home into the street; if the parents did not renounce Jesus Christ, their children were executed before their eyes. It was—and remains—horrible.

Those reports lingered in my mind as I reread an often-overlooked portion of the Christmas story:

> Herod was furious when he learned that the wise men had outwitted him. He sent soldiers to kill all the boys in and around Bethlehem who were two years old and under, because the wise men had told him the star first appeared to them about two years earlier. Herod's brutal action fulfilled the prophecy of Jeremiah: "A cry of anguish is heard in Ramah—weeping and mourning unrestrained. Rachel weeps for her children, refusing to be comforted—for they are dead." (Matt. 2:16–18 NLT)

The parallel is so stark I want to ask for a moment of silence.

I have never seen this part of the story portrayed in any Christmas pageant or manger scene. For many of us raised in middle America, this genocide was completely left out of our Christmas understanding. Our visions of the nativity were shaped by classic Christmas cards, and by the lovely crèche displays in parks, on church lawns, and on many coffee tables. And while I still love those tableaus very much, I am convinced they are an almost total rewrite of the story.

On the night before the "massacre of the innocents," another urgent moment took place:

> After the wise men were gone, an angel of the Lord appeared to Joseph in a dream. "Get up and flee to Egypt with the child and his mother," the angel said. "Stay there until I tell you to return, because Herod is going to try to kill the child." That night Joseph left for Egypt with the child and Mary, his mother, and they stayed there until Herod's death. (Matt. 2:13–15 NLT)

This, too, seems right out of the devastation in the Middle East—refugees fleeing for their lives, taking cover in a foreign country. But nor have I seen this portrayed in the lovely imagery surrounding Christmastime (not, at least, in the twentieth century; not in hometown American culture). I understand the imagery is dear to many of us, but it is also profoundly *deceiving*; it creates all sorts of warm feelings, associations, and expectations—many quite subconscious—of what the nature of the Christian life is going to be like for us. The omissions are, in fact, dangerous— the equivalent of ignoring the movements of ISIS.

That adolescent part of me says, "Wait a minute. God is almighty, omnipotent, ruler of a hundred billion galaxies; his power makes a nuclear meltdown a mere sneeze. His Son—and their plan to rescue the world—was in imminent danger. Why didn't God Almighty send his angel armies to protect young Jesus?" Indeed—why did an angel have to come in the middle of the night and whisk the holy family away in secrecy, hiding them south of the border? Herod and his secret police were nothing compared to the living God.

The story ought to make you wonder about your assumptions of what exactly is going on here, and how God works in the world. Certainly it ought to cause us to rethink our views on prayer. "I asked; he didn't move" seems grossly out of touch in light of these stories. Perhaps this account of prayer from the life of Daniel will help; it begins with prayer, and confusion: "In the third year of Cyrus king of Persia, a revelation was given to Daniel (who was called Belteshazzar). Its message was true and it concerned a great war" (Dan. 10:1).

Daniel is troubled, as any of us would be. *Why am I being given a vision about a great war? I wasn't looking for this. What can it mean?* So he devotes himself to prayer and fasting—for three weeks. That detail alone sets Daniel apart from most of us. The longest I have fasted is three days, and it almost took me out. On the twenty-first day of his vigil, Daniel is walking along the banks of the Tigris River in the ancient kingdom of Babylon; I like that—I like to walk as I pray. Suddenly, a real, live angel of God appears. We know he is real and very much alive because his presence is so overwhelming the men with Daniel are "filled with terror" and run for their lives. Daniel doesn't run; he can't even move; he is lying on his face, nearly in a trance (don't you love the gripping detail of these stories?):

A hand touched me and set me trembling on my hands and knees. He said, "Daniel, you who are highly esteemed, consider carefully the words I am about to speak to you, and stand up, for I have now been sent to you." And when he said this to me, I stood up trembling.

Then he continued, "Do not be afraid, Daniel. Since the first day that you set your mind to gain understanding and to humble yourself before your God, your words were heard, and I have come in response to them. But the prince of the Persian kingdom resisted me twenty-one days. Then Michael, one of the chief princes, came to help me, because I was detained there with the king of Persia. Now I have come to explain to you what will happen to your people in the future, for the vision concerns a time yet to come." (Dan. 10:10–14)

Did you follow that—God answered Daniel's prayers *the first day he prayed*. He even sent an angel to personally bring his reply. But the answer was delayed *for three weeks* because a mighty fallen angel, a demon with the rank of a principality, held the Persian kingdom (where Daniel lived) under his rule and barred the way. God's angel had to fight his way in, and at the end of their encounter he told Daniel he was going to have to fight his way back out.

The Scriptures are a sort of wake-up call to the human race, a trumpet blast, to use Francis Thompson's phrase, "from this hid battlements of eternity."[5] One alarm they repeatedly sound is that we are all caught up in the midst of a collision of kingdoms—the kingdom of God advancing with force against the kingdom of darkness, which for the moment holds most of the world in its clutches. Is this your understanding of the world you find yourself in? Does this shape the way you pray—and the way you interpret "unanswered" prayer?

Now yes, Jesus has come and that has changed everything. But maybe not like you think. The advent of Jesus at Christmastime accelerated the collision of kingdoms into global war:

A great and wondrous sign appeared in heaven: a woman clothed with the sun, with the moon under her feet and a crown of twelve stars on her head. She was pregnant and cried out in pain as she was about to give birth.

Then another sign appeared in heaven: an enormous red dragon with seven heads and ten horns and seven crowns on his heads. His tail swept a third of the stars out of the sky and flung them to the earth. The dragon stood in front of the woman who was about to give birth, so that he might devour her child the moment it was born.

She gave birth to a son, a male child, who will rule all the nations with an iron scepter . . .

And there was war in heaven. Michael and his angels fought against the dragon, and the dragon and his angels fought back. But he was not strong enough, and they lost their place in heaven. The great dragon was hurled down—that ancient serpent called the devil, or Satan, who leads the whole world astray. He was hurled to the earth, and his angels with him.

Then I heard a loud voice in heaven say:

"Now have come the salvation and the power and the
    kingdom of our God,
        and the authority of his Christ.
For the accuser of our brothers,
        who accuses them before our God day and night,
        has been hurled down.
They overcame him
        by the blood of the Lamb
        and by the word of their testimony;

> they did not love their lives so much
>> as to shrink from death.
> Therefore rejoice, you heavens
>> and you who dwell in them!
> But woe to the earth and the sea,
>> because the devil has gone down to you!
> He is filled with fury,
>> because he knows that his time is short . . ."

Then the dragon was enraged at the woman and went off to make war against the rest of her offspring—those who obey God's commandments and hold to the testimony of Jesus. (Rev. 12:1–5, 7–12, 17)

Look—you may not like the story you find yourself in, but your displeasure doesn't make it go away. If the execution of children by ISIS extremists doesn't clarify matters, I just don't know how much more evidence it is going to take to convince the church that we are at war. The dragon has declared war on all those who align themselves with Jesus. The moment we were born, we found ourselves in the midst of a fierce battle.

If this doesn't shape your understanding of the role of prayer, you *will* find yourself repeatedly disappointed and disheartened.

For one thing, prayer is not simply asking God to do stuff. Clearly.

Knowing this, can you begin to see why sweet, little "Jesus be with us" prayers are so grossly inadequate to our situation? Why Patch's understanding of the world is so utterly incomplete—and heartbreaking?

When Aslan lays his charge upon the children he loves, he is doing them a great honor. He knows what this will require. As did Jesus, when he said to his dear ones, "I am sending you out like sheep among wolves" (Matt. 10:16). The metaphor so perfectly describes our situation we almost want to smile—like when the young bride and groom are waving good-bye and the grandfather leans over to the grandmother and whispers, "They have no idea what they've just gotten themselves into." The humor of absurd understatement.

But sheep among wolves is, at the same time, so foreboding we decide not to think about it. Maybe he was just referring to the early disciples.

To Sum Up

We are trying to clear away mistaken assumptions about God and his world so that we can better understand prayer.

God is growing us all up.
We find ourselves in the midst of a great and terrible war.

Now, if I were him, I think I would have taken care of the first so that we could get on with the second. Let's get everyone whole and strong and filled with the power of God, and then we can take Normandy, spiritually speaking. Or, I'd maybe even prefer the reverse—overthrow the kingdom of darkness, rid the world of evil in one fell swoop, and then there will be breathing room to see humanity restored.

Because honestly, to conduct the invasion *while* God is still growing us up looks to me like hitting the beach at Normandy not with a battalion of marines, but with Mrs. Simpson's third-grade class, the junior high youth group from First Presbyterian, and a handful of adults chosen at random from the phone book. It looks like a hobbit with a handkerchief going to slay a dragon.

But I did not write this story, and the One who did hasn't consulted me on the matter.

So this is where we are—in precisely the same position Bilbo and the children in Narnia found themselves. (Perhaps that is why we love those stories; something deep inside knows it to be true.)

Now, if you believed both assumptions, if they were woven into your deepest convictions about the world, you would want to learn to pray like a soldier wants to learn to use his weapon, like a smoke jumper wants to learn survival skills. We really have no idea what sort of breakthrough is actually possible until we learn to pray. Perhaps we, too, will be ending droughts and stopping wildfires.

Three

THE CRY OF THE HEART

Yes, it had been raining, but we did not know about the hail. It was a freak of nature. One of those random western cloudbursts dumped a thousand frozen golf balls along a stretch of Highway 395 ten miles ahead, in preparation for our arrival. We were blasting south from Bridgeport, on our way home from a fishing trip, making time in my buddy Frank's '81 Ford Econoline—one of those big old vans preferred by churches and kidnappers.

We were going too fast, coming around that bend, and the hail appeared too quickly for any real reaction. "Whoa . . . what's that white stuff? . . . Is that *hail?*" But by then we were into our first 360, graceful as a figure skater, spinning over those big icy marbles into oncoming traffic and the irrigation ditch on the far side. The hippo ballerinas from *Fantasia* come to mind— behemoths cutting elegant turns as they spin and spin toward catastrophe. This took you longer to read than it took to happen.

I put my hand on the dashboard to brace for the flip I knew was coming, and prayed the only thing I could pray, the only thing I really needed to pray: *"Jesus!"*

Next thing I knew we were hanging upside down (seat belts do work), oil pouring in through the instrument panel, windshield wipers going *thump, thwack, thump, thwack* because who remembers to turn off the wipers after you've rolled your van? Our stunned silence was broken by spontaneous laughter, flowing from that giddy, light-headed relief that follows a near head-on.

Some prayers just happen; they are "the Cry of the Heart." No training is needed when it comes to this kind of prayer. I've uttered it thousands of times; I'm confident you have too. Like when the phone rings and the bad news starts to spill and all you can do is say, *Father . . . Father . . . Father,* your heart crying out to God. It's a beautiful expression of prayer, rising from the deep places in us, often unbidden, always welcome to his loving ears. The Psalms are filled with this emotive praying:

> I cried out to God for help;
>> I cried out to God to hear me.
>> When I was in distress, I sought the Lord. (77:1–2)

> Hear my cry, O God;
>> listen to my prayer.
> From the ends of the earth I call to you,
>> I call as my heart grows faint;
>> lead me to the rock that is higher than I.
>> For you have been my refuge,
>> a strong tower against the foe. (61:1–3)

> How long, O LORD? Will you forget me forever?
> How long will you hide your face from me?
> How long must I wrestle with my thoughts
>   and every day have sorrow in my heart?
> How long will my enemy triumph over me? (13:1–2)

Doesn't something within you resonate simply reading those words of the psalmist? Our soul responds, *Yes*. There is a kinship here. Words are being put to places we have known. Words like "distress" and "my heart grows faint" and "refuge" play like a bowstring on the cello of our hearts. As does, "how long?" I let go a deep sigh I didn't even know was there; I didn't know I was holding my breath in that way. "How long?" is a phrase you run into many places in the Psalms; it is so true to the human condition.

In fact, the honesty of these prayers are, for me, one of the proofs for the authenticity of the Bible. I mean, if you were going to try starting a religion and you needed to convince the world to join your cause, I doubt you'd be nearly as gritty as the Scriptures actually are. Nothing is cleaned up for the public here. Which is an enormous gift to us; there is permission here to have an emotional life, and to bring it all to God: "pour out your hearts to him, for God is our refuge" (Ps. 62:8).

The Cry of the Heart just comes, if you'll let it. These are the prayers I find myself already praying as I'm waking up in the morning. "O God—help. Help me today, Lord." Sometimes it's just one word, repeated in my heart: *Jesus, Jesus, Jesus*. I think it will just flow for you, too, if you give it permission. Turn the editor off; let your heart and soul speak. In the Psalms, David is clearly unedited, unrestrained. Good grief—he's all over the map. One moment it's "I love you, Lord!" and the next it's "Why have you forsaken me?"

> I will praise you, O LORD, with all my heart;
>> I will tell of all your wonders.
> I will be glad and rejoice in you;
>> I will sing praise to your name, O Most High. (9:1–2)

> My God, my God, why have you forsaken me?
>> Why are you so far from saving me,
>> so far from the words of my groaning? (22:1)

You almost wonder if it is the same person; I find myself giving a quick glance to the top of the psalm to see if this is still David speaking. And it is. He goes from his heart absolutely bursting with joy, to utter desolation:

> You have filled my heart with greater joy
>> than when their grain and new wine abound. (4:7)

> My soul is in anguish.
>> How long, O LORD, how long? (6:3)

One day he is writing ballads about the mighty victories of God; the next he is singing songs of lament and woe:

> How priceless is your unfailing love!
> Both high and low among men
>> find refuge in the shadow of your wings.
> They feast on the abundance of your house;

you give them drink from your river of delights.
(36:7–8)

My heart is in anguish within me;
the terrors of death assail me. (55:4)

David's graphic confessions of sin and its ravages are among the most poignant in the literature of the world:

My guilt has overwhelmed me
like a burden too heavy to bear.
My wounds fester and are loathsome
because of my sinful folly.
I am bowed down and brought very low;
all day long I go about mourning.
My back is filled with searing pain;
there is no health in my body.
I am feeble and utterly crushed;
I groan in anguish of heart.
All my longings lie open before you, O Lord;
my sighing is not hidden from you.
My heart pounds, my strength fails me;
even the light has gone from my eyes. (38:4–10)

That humility soon vanishes, and he is crying out to God to bring apocalypse down on his enemies:

The righteous will be glad when they are avenged,
when they bathe their feet in the blood of the wicked.
(58:10)

Good heavens. He certainly isn't embarrassed by the world reading his journals; nothing is hidden here. David quite lustily sails the seven seas of human emotion in his prayers. You couldn't get away with this in most churches. The man seems reckless, unstable; your average board of trustees would have him sent to a therapist. But remember—David is called a man after God's own heart. It was *God* who made him king and canonized his prayers in the Bible. These psalms are given to the church as our prayer book, our primer, and they are beautiful. Assuring us that not only can God handle the full span of our emotional life, he *invites us* to bring it to him.

There was another man who learned these lessons well, a man in the line of David who clearly studied his primer. The unbridled strength of the psalms resounds in the prayers of Jesus; listen to this description I found buried in the book of Hebrews: "During the days of Jesus' life on earth, he offered up prayers and petitions with loud cries and tears to the one who could save him from death" (Heb. 5:7).

My prayers don't sound like that; they are not loud, and only on rare occasion are they accompanied by tears. Yet here is Jesus—the best man of all, "more human than humanity" as G. K. Chesterton said.[1] Here is how he prayed. I don't believe Gethsemane was the only time his disciples witnessed it—we have the account at Lazarus's tomb as well. But of course our thoughts turn to that famous grove of olive trees and the midnight vigil held there:

> Then Jesus went with his disciples to a place called Gethsemane, and he said to them, "Sit here while I go over there and pray."
> He took Peter and the two sons of Zebedee along with him,

and he began to be sorrowful and troubled. Then he said to them, "My soul is overwhelmed with sorrow to the point of death. Stay here and keep watch with me."

Going a little farther, he fell with his face to the ground and prayed . . .

And being in anguish, he prayed more earnestly, and his sweat was like drops of blood falling to the ground. (Matt. 26:36–39; Luke 22:44)

I find myself embarrassed by how "formal" my prayer life has become, how careful. As I read the Psalms and watch Jesus pray, I realize I am not allowing my heart's full range of emotion to express itself in my prayers, as if I have to somehow shield God from the full depth of the seas within me. There was a time in my life when my prayers sounded more like David's, or Jesus'.

A dear friend of mine had been killed in an accident, and there was no careful praying in the days that followed. I kicked a hole in the wall of the kitchen while praying. Fearful I would bring down the whole house, I would go out to the garage and take a baseball bat to a large plastic trash can in prayer: *"What are you thinking?!"* I would yell, with tears. *"How could you do this?!"* (I kept the door closed so as not to alarm the neighbors.) It was, without question, the most honest time of prayer in my life.

E. M. Bounds, that legendary nineteenth-century prophet of prayer, wrote, "The entire man must pray. The whole man—life, heart, temper, mind, are in it . . . it takes a whole heart to do effectual praying."[2] The whole man was involved in those prayers of mine in the garage. They were my Cry of the Heart.

But over the years I toned it down; I became more . . . I dunno, reverent? Careful? It seems silly even to write those words, but my prayers weren't loud and they no longer came with tears. So I decided that if God could handle David's full range of emotion, he could handle mine. (Really, I think we have this feeling that we have to hide most of us when we come to God in prayer, like a child tries to hide the mess he's made as he comes to his mother's call, even though she sees his muddy jeans. As if God doesn't already know.) I began to take the editor off and let my prayers just flow up from my heart. It was a really good shift. Not only did I feel far more connected to God, my heart to his, but my prayers took on a whole new power as well. The old saints called it "unction"; it's a word that means "oomph." These prayers had oomph.

Now, let me be quick to say, the Cry of the Heart is not only cries of heartache. It is not even primarily cries of sorrow or distress. It includes all sorts of joyful spontaneity and triumph as well. Joy can be "loud" too:

> Clap your hands, all you nations;
>> shout to God with cries of joy. (Ps. 47:1)

> My lips will shout for joy
>> when I sing praise to you. (Ps. 71:23)

> Come, let us sing for joy to the LORD;
>> let us shout aloud to the Rock of our salvation. (Ps. 95:1)

In fact, "shout to the Lord" is used many times in the Psalms. Do you shout in your prayers? It will get you closer to Jesus' prayers, which were *loud*, may I remind you. You probably do this already—like when good news suddenly appears; when the doctor gives you a clean bill of health; when you land the big promotion; when you're skiing, sailing, or on the downhill rush of the roller coaster. *Whoop!* You just didn't know you were doing it "unto the Lord." But the Cry of the Heart is right there, and he loves it. I'm certain God and the angels shout right along with you.

As Stasi and I have left behind the careful prayers of a quiet chapel, the music decibel has gone through the roof at our house in the last few years; we *crank* the worship, accompanied by all sorts of spontaneous whoops and hollers. (The neighbors must think we have slipped the rails.)

The Cry of the Heart is not something you have to arrange for, or practice, or even learn. It doesn't require religious language. You do not have to kneel or close your eyes (and a good thing, too, because most of my praying takes place in the car or as I'm out walking in the woods). There needs to be nothing formal about it at all; in fact, do everything you possibly can to get rid of all formality, all those "thees" and "thous" and religious posturing.

Just give it permission. Those prayers are in there.

Now for a word of caution: be careful that your heart-cries do not subtly turn into *agreements* with despair or forsakenness. Do not let "Father—I feel abandoned!" turn into an agreement with, "I *am* abandoned." It is such a relief to admit the anguish, but in this post-postmodern hour, where the minor theme of suffering and desolation has become the major theme, it is too easy to "land" in a place of heartache and call it authenticity. The emotions are real, and they matter, but emotions are not a safe harbor for the soul. Our enemy is always there in times of distress, trying to get us to agree with his lies, *You are forsaken.*

33

The child who cries out in the dark feels very differently when Mother comes in and switches on a light. What felt so real and inevitable vanishes. Let us be careful we don't embrace the pain in such a way that we forbid God to turn on the light and draw near. Watch how David handles the stormy waters of his own soul:

> My tears have been my food
>> day and night,
> while men say to me all day long,
>> "Where is your God?"
> These things I remember
>> as I pour out my soul:
> how I used to go with the multitude,
>> leading the procession to the house of God,
> with shouts of joy and thanksgiving
>> among the festive throng.
> Why are you downcast, O my soul?
>> Why so disturbed within me?
> Put your hope in God,
>> for I will yet praise him,
>> my Savior and my God. (Ps. 42:3–6)

He admits it, he pours it all out with raw honesty, *but he does not allow himself to stay there.* Don't you love it that David talks to himself ("Why are you downcast, O my soul?")? That makes me feel a little more sane because I talk to myself all the time. He reminds his own soul that things have not always been like this— and isn't that where we begin to make the fatal shift? When we are in the darkness, we begin to feel like we have always been there. *But it is not true.* David reminds himself that God has been faithful

34

in the past; God will be faithful again. He urges himself to put his hope in God because the morning *will* come.

The Cry of the Heart is a beautiful and precious form of prayer. But there is a danger to it (just as romance and friendship have their dangers). The honest release of emotion can at times become a whirlpool that sucks you in. I'm trying to keep you from making agreements while you give yourself permission to have a full, emotional life with God. "I feel forsaken!" is very, very different from "I *am* forsaken!" "I feel overcome" is much different than "I *am* overcome."

Notice how David escapes the shipwreck of the soul: he turns his attention from the debris of his life in a much healthier direction; he turns his gaze toward *God*.

I called the Psalms our primer when it comes to prayer, and I did mean *primer*; there is more to learn, and far more effective prayers to pray. We live in a very different moment in the story than David and his colleagues; a great deal has changed since the Psalms were penned. The incarnation, for one thing—the Son of God has come. Your ransom, for another. The cross has happened, the resurrection too. Tectonic shifts have shaken the heavens and the earth, and those events change the posture of our praying in profound ways.

The Cry of the Heart is one form of prayer, and a beautiful one. But there is another, far more intentional, where we take up sword and shield and start changing the course of events through strong, determined prayer—the Prayer of Intervention. Prayer that stops wildfires, prayer that ends droughts. We'll begin to explore that next.

Four

WHO HE IS AND WHO WE ARE

One exhortation of Scripture I long to keep far better than I do is this wonderful charge: "Therefore, since we are surrounded by such a great cloud of witnesses, let us throw off everything that hinders and the sin that so easily entangles, and let us run with perseverance the race marked out for us. Let us fix our eyes on Jesus, the author and perfecter of our faith" (Heb. 12:1–2).

As I fight my way through the battles of this world, my eyes aren't normally fixed on Jesus. I do look his direction more than I used to, but far more often my eyes are fixed on the crises before me. They have a way of arresting my attention.

A dear friend is currently in a heinous battle with cancer. It has been waged over years now, and I cannot tell if we are in the final hours or not. Only God knows the number of prayers that have gone up for him; it feels like the number of stars in the heavens. This morning we received a turn of bad news and immediately went to prayer. But I did not feel confident and assured; I certainly did not feel triumphant. I wasn't expecting a cloud the size of a man's fist rising from the sea. I felt discouraged and distressed—my gaze was fixed on his suffering, not upon the resources of the living God.

And oh, what a difference it makes.

There is a beautiful scene in the third of the Hobbit trilogy of films, *The Battle of the Five Armies.* The dwarves (and Bilbo) have in fact awakened the dragon, Smaug, from his slumbers; the beast is enraged that anyone would dare challenge his stolen kingdom. Lashing out with indiscriminate vengeance, Smaug swoops down upon the unsuspecting village of Lake-town, breathing fire and death with every pass. In moments the wooden township is engulfed in flames. One man dares to rise against him—the bowman Bard. While the hamlet rages and the rest of the townsfolk flee, Bard climbs to the top of the bell tower and begins to fire arrows as the murderous beast passes by. But the armor of Smaug is impenetrable, "like tenfold shields," save only by a black arrow from the elder days.

Bard's son Bain knows this, and he knows where the last black arrow lies hidden. As Bard takes his final shot and the wooden arrow bounces off the dragon's armor, Bain appears in the tower with what might be a miracle. Smaug detects the movement, and while the inferno that was once Lake-town rages all 'round him, the scaled malice turns his full attention on the two figures in the tower . . .

"Is that your child?" [The bloody monster licks his lips as he advances.] "You cannot save him from the fire . . . he will *burn!*"

37

[Father and son are working together; Bard is using Bain's shoulder as a rest while he aims the black arrow for the one chink in Smaug's armor. Smaug is coming on with dreadful finality.]

"Tell me, wretch, how now do you challenge *me?* You have nothing left but your death."

[The dragon's roar shakes the timbers and the marrow in their bones; he is coming on like the Day of Judgment. Bain turns to look at the advancing monster. Then, a calm and reassuring voice says . . .]

"Bain! Look at me—you look at me."[1]

The boy turns his gaze from the nightmare to his father's loving face, and my heart sees myself in him, sees the answer to all my fears. I've watched the scene several times now, and I think of Jesus—this was the secret to his prayers:

Taking the five loaves and the two fish *and looking up to heaven*, he gave thanks and broke the loaves. Then he gave them to his disciples to set before the people. He also divided the two fish among them all. They all ate and were satisfied, and the disciples picked up twelve basketfuls of broken pieces of bread and fish. The number of the men who had eaten was five thousand. (Mark 6:41–44, emphasis added)

Jesus, once more deeply moved, came to the tomb. It was a cave with a stone laid across the entrance. "Take away the stone," he said.

"But, Lord," said Martha, the sister of the dead man, "by this time there is a bad odor, for he has been there four days."

Then Jesus said, "Did I not tell you that if you believed, you would see the glory of God?"

So they took away the stone. *Then Jesus looked up* and said, "Father, I thank you that you have heard me. I knew that you always hear me, but I said this for the benefit of the people standing here, that they may believe that you sent me."

When he had said this, Jesus called in a loud voice, "Lazarus, come out!" The dead man came out, his hands and feet wrapped with strips of linen, and a cloth around his face.

Jesus said to them, "Take off the grave clothes and let him go." (John 11:38–44, emphasis added)

Jesus is not looking up like a man trying to recall something he just forgot. He looks up to heaven to fix his attention on his Father's loving face. He is orienting himself to what is most true in the world—not the impossibly inadequate resources for the need of the five thousand, not the sister's grief (they were his dear friends), not even the finality of death sealed with a stone rolled over the tomb. He turns his gaze from all that "evidence" and fixes it upon his Father God and the resources of his kingdom.

We know that faith plays a critical role in effective praying— maybe *the* critical role—and so we feel that somehow we have to generate faith. That never works, nor does it help to try and generate *feelings* of faith. We must look from the debris to God. Peter looks at Christ, and he can walk on the water; he looks at the waves, and he goes down.

Agnes Sanford was a woman with a remarkable gift of physical healing; many miracles were confirmed at her hands. I found it extremely insightful that when praying for sick children, she would often ask the parents to leave the room, the reason being that the fears and anxieties of the parents were actually getting in the way of effective prayer—just as anxiety gets in the way of a good night's sleep, just as anger gets in the way of a reconciling conversation. The parents were fixed upon their child's suffering, and therefore they were impotent in prayer; Agnes fixed upon God, and her prayers were mighty.

Before we can learn the Prayer of Intervention, we must clarify who we are, and Who we are praying to—or *with*. For as we saw with Elijah, effective prayer is far more a partnership with God than it is begging him to do something.

God

I am using a computer to write this book; it sits on my desk in my home office. The wallpaper on my computer—the background image that fills the entire screen—is a gorgeous photo of a piece of ocean and rugged coastline in Ireland. Our family spent an idyllic summer holiday there. One look at this photo and I am reminded of everything I know to be true about God: *he is the creator of everything I love.* Waterfalls, mountains, wild places; rivers, forests, sunshine, the night sky; beauty, goodness, truth.

Just start there—think of all the things you love in this world. And then remind yourself that the God you are praying to is the one who made them all. It helps me to hold and touch and feel something in the natural world—a leaf, a stone. I love placing my palm on the surface of the flowing water of a stream and reminding myself, *God did this; he is immensely powerful, creative, generous, and intimate.* You are talking to an immensely powerful, creative, generous, and intimate Person when you talk to God:

"With my great power and outstretched arm I made the earth and its people and the animals that are on it" (Jer. 27:5).

I'll pause sometimes and wonder over the eye of our golden retriever, or one of our horses. The eye is utterly astounding—it enables you to *see*, for heaven's sake. But it is also elegant, and exquisitely made, with the dappled-colored beauty of the iris, the pupil so deep and mysterious, like "the pools of Heshbon" as Solomon captured it (Song 7:4). The eye of a horse is so large it is startling, its pupil so deep it looks like you could view the kingdom of God in it, like the hermit's pool in C. S. Lewis's *The Horse and His Boy*. And despite all its achievements, science has not been able to make a lens that can do what the eye can do.

Then I think of the sunlight that enables our eyes to take in the beauty of the world around us; isn't sunlight wonderful? I'm one of those folks easily affected by seasonal mood disorder; a few cloudy days and I'm feeling a bit overcast myself. Then the sun breaks out and bathes the world in gold and I'm happy as a leprechaun. Don't you just love the sun? The way it causes the night to flee, and the grass to grow, the trees to leaf out, the flowers to burst into bloom? Don't you love the way it warms you after a plunge into a cold pool or stream? (I am trying to remind myself just Who this person is I'm praying to.)

> In the heavens he has pitched a tent for the sun,
>> which is like a bridegroom coming forth from his
>>> pavilion,
>> like a champion rejoicing to run his course.
> It rises at one end of the heavens
>> and makes its circuit to the other;
>> nothing is hidden from its heat. (Ps. 19:4–6)

God gave us *the sun*—this ought to answer any doubts about his power and goodness. All life on this planet derives its life from the sun, that celestial nuclear device with a surface temperature of 5,500 Celsius. Our mothers told us never to look directly at it, but when you sneak a peek, it appears to be the diameter of a pencil eraser. Yet more than a million earths could fit inside the sun. Inconceivable amounts of energy are generated at its core, as hydrogen converts to helium by nuclear fusion. One solar flare releases more energy than ten *million* volcanoes. (This is helping me realize God is powerful enough for whatever need I am praying over.)

Now get this—there are roughly one hundred billion stars of all sizes in a galaxy, and one hundred billion galaxies in the universe. Which means there are approximately four hundred billion billion suns like ours that God has made. If you began counting to that number today, you could not finish the task in your lifetime. Meanwhile, God is providing the energy of those suns every moment. J. B. Phillips nailed the predicament of too many Christians: "Your God is too small."[2]

Words seem ridiculous at this point, but let us say clearly: Power is not an issue with God. His resources are unlimited. Is this the Person you have in mind as you pray? You must turn your gaze in the direction of God, or something that reminds you just who he is.

One of the reasons I love flying over the ocean is that it speaks to me of the vast abundance of God. The trans-Atlantic flight from Miami to Johannesburg is seventeen hours—hours and hours spent passing over the vast expanse of the ocean. Think of the volume of water down there. Like four hundred billion billion suns, this was the very lesson Jesus was trying to get across to his disciples—drive home with visual impact—when he fed the five thousand with a few loaves and fishes. *His resources are unlimited.*

I also need to remind myself that God *reigns*.

One of the subtle, crippling effects of an Internet world is that we are aware of every atrocity within moments of its occurrence, any place in the world. The earthquake that killed hundreds of thousands in Haiti, the millions of children in the sex trade. Such news is not benign; it has an *effect* on us. The evil one pounces, poisoning our confidence that a good and loving God is in control. As a friend said at lunch yesterday, "It takes everything to believe that God exists and that he's good." And he was simply talking about the pain in one person's life.

David described this tension in the Psalms—the people around him were freaking out over the "ISIS" of their day. He countered by stubbornly clinging to what he knew was true of God:

> In the LORD I take refuge.
>> How then can you say to me:
>> "Flee like a bird to your mountain.
> For look, the wicked bend their bows;
>> they set their arrows against the strings
> to shoot from the shadows
>> at the upright in heart.
> When the foundations are being destroyed,
>> what can the righteous do?"
> The LORD is in his holy temple;
>> the LORD is on his heavenly throne. (11:1–4)

He refused to let current events move him from the eternal

fact that God reigns. The kingly reign of the Lord God Almighty is the "still point of the turning world," to borrow T. S. Eliot's beautiful phrase; it is the fixed point of the Scriptures:[3]

> The LORD reigns, he is robed in majesty;
>> the LORD is robed in majesty
>> and is armed with strength.
> The world is firmly established;
>> it cannot be moved.
> Your throne was established long ago;
>> you are from all eternity. (93:1–2)

I think my heart's need to be assured of this is the reason I love this description of Jesus: "The Son is the radiance of God's glory and the exact representation of his being, sustaining all things by his powerful word" (Heb. 1:3). Or as the New Living Translation says, "He sustains the universe by the mighty power of his command."

Look—if God were to lose control of the worlds he made, nature would be collapsing into utter chaos all around you. Planets would be colliding; earthquakes would be leveling civilization; matter itself would be coming unglued (scientists still have no idea what holds all matter together). Some*one* is holding this all together, "sustaining" it by his command. The sun came up again this morning; I am able to breathe because oxygen is still in generous supply; the law of gravity is still in effect; the ocean is still filled with water; matter is still being held together. If the enemy had truly gained the upper hand, we would all be dead by now and the earth an ashen wasteland. The fact that you are here, reading this book right now in this moment—with your eyes working and your mind perceiving, the room filled with air and the ground beneath you fixed in place—is proof enough that God maintains control over the universe.

Who are you praying to? Is he adequate? Is he kind? Is he in a good mood? Where is he located? Is he near or far away?

Sometimes I catch myself praying to the "sky God," thinking he is somewhere up there, above us, beyond the wild blue yonder. This sneaks into our assumptions; like Bette Midler sang, God watches us—"from a distance."[4] It might sound reverent, but it is *disheartening*; he seems so far away. I know the Bible speaks of God enthroned in the heavens, but we have projected our own ideas into that and assumed that means "way up there somewhere." Yet Scripture presents him right at your elbow:

> He is not far from each one of us. "For in him we live and move and have our being." (Acts 17:27–28)

God is *near*; he is close; he is all around us. I like letting other translations deepen and enrich my understanding:

> He doesn't play hide-and-seek with us. He's not remote; he's *near*. We live and move in him, can't get away from him! (MSG)

> He is not far from any one of us. For in him we live and move and exist. (NLT)

So when Thomas à Kempis said, "When Jesus is near, all is well and nothing seems difficult. When He is absent, all is hard," I believe what he meant was, *When we are aware of how near Jesus is*, all is well and nothing seems difficult.[5] *When He seems absent,* all is hard. For he never, ever leaves us. That is why the old priest urged us to, "Fix your mind on the Most High, and pray unceasingly to Christ."[6]

Most of all, above every other reminder, as you turn your gaze to God in prayer, what is your heart's conviction on *his* heart—is he loving?

Oh, how it helps me to remind myself, *I am praying to the One who gave his life for me.* When we look to the stormy seas of our circumstances to try and assure ourselves God is loving, we are fighting a losing battle. That is why we have to go to the true "fixed point" in the universe—the man hanging in execution on Calvary's hilltop.

> You see, at just the right time, when we were still powerless, Christ died for the ungodly. Very rarely will anyone die for a righteous man, though for a good man someone might possibly dare to die. But God demonstrates his own love for us in this: While we were still sinners, Christ died for us. (Rom. 5:6–8)

This resolves the issue in a way nothing else can remotely touch or settle. You should not, must not, please, please do not evaluate the loving-kindness of God toward you by the swirling tornado of events—*especially by whether or not he seems to be answering the prayer at hand.* Your heart cannot take such abuse; you will find yourself swirling around like Dorothy in a Kansas cyclone, debris flying this way and that. It will leave you exhausted, uncertain, fearful, and desolate after a few months, let alone years.

I am praying to the One who gave his life for me. Just let your heart linger there for a moment; picture the event in your mind. *I am praying to the One who gave his life for me.* You will feel confidence in talking to him, assurance that he cares more about what you care about than you do. (Parents—do you feel that God loves your children more than you do? Or your friends? Your dearest?) If this was the Person I had clearly in mind, clearly in my heart as I prayed, I know it would make a world of difference. I would be so confident; I would expect good things; I would feel triumphant right from the start. And *that* is why we are urged to "fix our eyes" on Jesus—especially as we pray.

This immensely powerful, creative, generous, intimate, and loving Person also happens to be your Father. Which brings us to our situation in the prayer relationship.

And You?

A man I counseled years ago described his childhood with such a stark image it stayed with me like a metaphor. The story went like this: His father was a very successful man; he left for work before the boy woke in the morning and returned home just in time for dinner. After their rather efficient meal his father would disappear behind a closed door into his home office, working there late into the night. This was his daily routine. The boy—longing for his father's affection—would sit in the hallway outside his father's office, writing little notes to his father and pushing them under the crack in the door. "I always hoped that one time, just once, he would pass a note back under the door to me. But he never did."

A heartbreaking story but an even more heartbreaking metaphor, for this is how many people conceive of their relationship with God—a busy man they hate to bother, whose affection they long for, passing their prayers under his door, hoping for just a word in return.

Honestly, when I listen to people pray (and nothing reveals your true beliefs like how you pray), more often than not it sounds like an orphan, crying for mercy outside the gates. "God, please . . . pleeease help me."

Just as we have to be careful to keep in mind exactly who it is we are praying to, what our images of God actually are, it is equally important to keep clear who *we* are in this process. Who are you to God? What is your relationship to the One to whom you pray? How do you conceive of it? Set aside your doctrine for a moment—what is your heart's settled assurance on the matter?

I said earlier that tectonic shifts have taken place in the universe since the Psalms were written; those shifts have forever changed your status with God and with his kingdom:

For you did not receive a spirit that makes you a slave again to fear, but you received the Spirit of sonship. And by him we cry, "Abba, Father." (Rom. 8:15)

But when the time had fully come, God sent his Son, born of a woman, born under law, to redeem those under law, that we might receive the full rights of sons.

Because you are sons, God sent the Spirit of his Son into our hearts, the Spirit who calls out, "Abba, Father." So you are no longer a slave, but a son; and since you are a son, God has made you also an heir. (Gal. 4:4–7)

Yes, yes—we have all heard that we are God's children; we are sons and daughters. The curse of familiarity with the words has dulled us to the staggering truth they contain. The reality of it has not penetrated our hearts, not deeply enough. We still act and pray like orphans or slaves.

A slave feels reluctant to pray; they feel they have no right to ask, and so their prayers are modest and respectful. They spend more time asking forgiveness than they do praying for abundance. They view the relationship with reverence, maybe more like fear, but not with the tenderness of love. Of *being* loved. There is no intimacy in the language or their feelings. Sanctified unworthiness colors their view of prayer. These are often "good servants of the Lord."

An orphan is not reluctant to pray; they feel desperate. But their prayers feel more like begging than anything else. Orphans feel a great chasm between themselves and the One to whom they speak. Abundance is a foreign concept; a poverty mentality permeates their prayer lives. They ask for scraps; they expect scraps.

But not sons; sons know who they are.

Mine were just home for Christmas, all three of them. They are young men now, out making their way in the world. And as is fitting to their stage in life, they are living on limited means. But when they come home, they get to feast. The refrigerator and pantry are theirs to pillage and they don't have to ask permission. When we go out to dinner, there is no question that Dad will take care of the bill. For they are sons—they get to live under their father's blessing; they get to drink from the abundance of my house (Ps. 36:8). And when the holidays were over and they packed up and left, they took with them my best shoes, my best sunglasses, some of my favorite books, climbing gear, and cigars—*with my absolute pleasure and blessing*. Luke was the last to go; he was hoping to pillage some of my travel gear for an upcoming trip. I said, "You are my son—everything I have is yours. Plunder as you will."

This is how sons get to live; this is how a father feels toward his sons.

With that in mind, listen to Jesus reframe our understanding of prayer. First, he uses a metaphor, like the story I just gave you about my sons. It is a story about a wayward son who breaks his father's heart by wandering off into a life of hedonism and self-destruction. Read this as if he were talking about you, for this is your story:

> After he had gone through all his money, there was a bad famine all through that country and he began to hurt. He signed on with a citizen there who assigned him to his fields to slop the pigs. He was so hungry he would have eaten the corncobs in the pig slop, but no one would give him any.
>
> That brought him to his senses. He said, "All those farmhands working for my father sit down to three meals a day, and here I am starving to death. I'm going back to my father. I'll say to him, Father, I've sinned against God, I've sinned before you; I don't deserve to be called your son. Take me on as a hired hand." He got right up and went home to his father.
>
> When he was still a long way off, his father saw him. His heart pounding, he ran out, embraced him, and kissed him. The son started his speech: "Father, I've sinned against God, I've sinned before you; I don't deserve to be called your son ever again."
>
> But the father wasn't listening. He was calling to the servants, "Quick. Bring a clean set of clothes and dress him. Put the family ring on his finger and sandals on his feet. Then get a

grain-fed heifer and roast it. We're going to feast! We're going to have a wonderful time! My son is here—given up for dead and now alive! Given up for lost and now found!" And they began to have a wonderful time. (Luke 15:14–24 MSG)

First off, did you notice the mentality of the son—did you hear the orphan and slave in him? He has a prayer "speech" all figured out; orphans and slaves make prayer speeches—they don't expect a two-way intimacy. Notice that his speech begins, "I don't deserve . . ."

But now look at things from the father's point of view: How can he see his son from "a long way off" unless he was first *looking* for his son? He can't see the boy from inside the house, behind a closed door; he must have been out on the porch, searching the horizon for the first glimpse of the returning boy. Do you come to prayer knowing that God is already expecting you, looking for you with longing?

The father *runs* to his son, embraces him, kisses him. This is how the father feels about you—the embrace, the kiss, all of it. I want to come to my father in prayer expecting an embrace. Don't you?

Of course, the older brother is upset by such lavish, *scandalous* generosity (and the truth of our position with God is so lavish, and so scandalous). As the story continues, the father goes outside to assure him, "My son . . . everything I have is yours" (v. 31).

Luke—everything I have is yours. Sons and daughters, everything God has is yours. Is that how you pray? On the night of his arrest, Jesus wanted to make sure his disciples understood this as well: "I tell you the truth, my Father will give you whatever you ask in my name. Until now you have not asked for anything in my name. Ask and you will receive, and your joy will be complete . . . I am not saying that I will ask the Father on your behalf. No, the Father himself loves you" (John 16:23–27).

He said, "Look—you don't need for me to ask on your behalf; my Father, who is now *your* Father, he loves you." And how does the Father love us? "I have made you [Father] known to them, and will continue to make you known in order that the love you have for me may be in them and that I myself may be in them" (John 17:26).

The Father loves you like he loves Jesus. Is this in your mind and heart as you come to prayer? You are not an orphan. You are not merely a "servant" of God. You are a son or daughter. And with that comes *privileges*: "But when the time had fully come, God sent his Son, born of a woman, born under law, to redeem those under law, that we might receive the full rights of sons" (Gal. 4:4–5).

I doubt any of us have tapped into that yet—the *full rights* as a son or daughter. Oh my. I have friends who pray with such confidence, and to be honest, their prayers are seeing greater results than mine. I think so much of it has to do with *expectation*; they are expecting the lavish and scandalous.

Friends and Allies

We are moving in this book toward an entirely different way of praying. To prepare ourselves, we are re-conceiving what our thoughts of God are like and how we see ourselves in the relationship. Dallas Willard said that we ought to look at our lives with God as a partnership. Not as needy, coming to the Lord of the universe hoping for some help, but as partners in a shared mission. This is how Jesus wanted us to see it: "Greater love has no one than this, that he lay down his life for his friends. You are my friends if you do what I command. I no longer call you servants, because a servant does not know his master's business. Instead, I have called you friends, for everything that I learned from my Father I have made known to you" (John 15:13–15).

Not only a son or daughter, you are also a friend of God—his confidant, his ally in bringing about his work on this earth.

By way of example, take healing prayer and the laying on of hands. We are instructed in James, in Hebrews, and by example in many other places that for physical healing, we are to lay hands on someone and pray for him. Now why is that—is it merely a gesture of kindness or comfort? No doubt it is both kind and comforting, but that is not why we are instructed in this procedure. Recall the story of the woman with the issue of blood:

> As Jesus was on his way, the crowds almost crushed him. And a woman was there who had been subject to bleeding for twelve years, but no one could heal her. She came up behind him and touched the edge of his cloak, and immediately her bleeding stopped.
>
> "Who touched me?" Jesus asked.
>
> When they all denied it, Peter said, "Master, the people are crowding and pressing against you."
>
> But Jesus said, "Someone touched me; I know that power has gone out from me." (Luke 8:42–46)

She was healed through physical contact because, as Jesus felt, "power has gone out from me." That's the purpose for laying on hands—so that the power of God can flow through you to the sick person's body. Yes, healing can come in other ways, but it primarily comes through the laying on of hands, illustrating how we are *partners* with God in prayer. His power is available; the need is there. What is needed is a *conduit*—a vessel through which God can work.

We see the same "partnership" idea in the story of Ananias praying for Saul (who would soon become Paul):

In Damascus there was a disciple named Ananias. The Lord called to him in a vision, "Ananias!"

"Yes, Lord," he answered.

The Lord told him, "Go to the house of Judas on Straight Street and ask for a man from Tarsus named Saul, for he is praying. In a vision he has seen a man named Ananias come and place his hands on him to restore his sight."

"Lord," Ananias answered, "I have heard many reports about this man and all the harm he has done to your saints in Jerusalem. And he has come here with authority from the chief priests to arrest all who call on your name." But the Lord said to Ananias, "Go! This man is my chosen instrument to carry my name before the Gentiles and their kings and before the people of Israel. I will show him how much he must suffer for my name."

Then Ananias went to the house and entered it. Placing his hands on Saul, he said, "Brother Saul, the Lord—Jesus, who appeared to you on the road as you were coming here— has sent me so that you may see again and be filled with the Holy Spirit."

Immediately, something like scales fell from Saul's eyes,

and he could see again. He got up and was baptized, and after taking some food, he regained his strength. (Acts 9:10–19)

The God of four hundred billion billion suns could certainly just give Paul back his sight—*zap*. But he insisted on using Ananias. What I love about the story is not only the miracle but the relationship Ananias has with Jesus—notice his comfort level in *arguing* with Jesus about the plan(!). You get the impression Ananias and Jesus are friends, comrades, partners in this young revolution called Christianity.

What Are You Looking At?

It is human nature to look at the problem before us, the crisis that has caused us to pray. But the problem is exactly the thing we should *not* be looking at.

You will want to have something before you that helps you turn your gaze from the wreckage to God. I respect the Orthodox church's use of icons; they are not meant to be understood as "pictures" of Jesus, but rather more like "symbols" that help the believer turn his or her attention to him. Better than looking at the stain in the carpet or the tiles on your ceiling. What will help you keep your eyes "fixed" on the truth of God? C. S. Lewis had only one picture on the walls of his bedroom—a photo of the image of Jesus' face from the Shroud of Turin. He would gaze upon it as he prayed.

I believe that as we grow in "fixing our gaze on Jesus," we can learn to turn our inner eyes to him and actually see him. As Pascal said, "It is the heart which experiences God."[7] But I'm not proficient at that, so I have a journal I keep in front of me—not a diary, but a journal of key truths I must remind myself of on a daily basis. That he is the God of four hundred billion billion suns. The creator of everything I love. That I am his son; I have the full rights of a son. It helps me get into the right frame of mind as I pray.

But, you may be thinking, *I try to think of myself as a son or daughter of a good and loving father when I pray; it doesn't seem to change the results.* That can be disheartening. But remember—we are not sitting on the back porch with our papa, drinking lemonade. We are heirs to the throne, joining our Father and Jesus on the field of battle. An invasion is underway.

Five

BOLD AUTHORITY

Why do we pray, "in Jesus' name"?

The phrase gets tacked onto the end of many prayers, but I think it has about as much meaning to us as "amen." Amen does not mean, "That's it . . . I'm done now," the little period at the end of my prayer. Amen (ah-mane) is an ancient Hebrew word that was transliterated (kept virtually intact) into New Testament Greek. It is a pronouncement, firm and authoritative: "Yes! So be it! Let this be done!" Amen is a declaration; in that sense it is like a command. Or it once was; now it has the emotional force of "talk to you later" at the end of a phone call.

"In Jesus' name" is even more of a command—far, far more declarative and final, like the drop of a judge's gavel. We are using the authority of the ruler of all galaxies and realms to *enforce* the power of what we have just prayed. We have been exploring the way things work in effective prayer; as we look deeper into the spiritual realm, we discover that the whole thing runs on authority.

It is the secret to the kingdom of God, and one of the essential secrets to prayer that works.

> When Jesus had entered Capernaum, a centurion came to him, asking for help. "Lord," he said, "my servant lies at home paralyzed and in terrible suffering."
>
> Jesus said to him, "I will go and heal him."
>
> The centurion replied, "Lord, I do not deserve to have you come under my roof. But just say the word, and my servant will be healed. For I myself am a man under authority, with soldiers under me. I tell this one, 'Go,' and he goes; and that one, 'Come,' and he comes. I say to my servant, 'Do this,' and he does it." When Jesus heard this, he was astonished and said to those following him, "I tell you the truth, I have not found anyone in Israel with such great faith." (Matt. 8:5–10)

I'm guessing it took something pretty remarkable to "astonish" Jesus (he was astonished). Did you notice what it was? The centurion understood *authority*.

> Just say the word from where you are, and my servant will be healed! I know, because I am under the authority of my superior officers and I have authority over my soldiers. I only need to say, "Go," and they go, or "Come," and they come. (vv. 8–9 NLT)

Remember—there is a way things work. If you run your hand along the grain of a 2x4, you'll get a splinter. If you approach an elk upwind, you'll spook him. If you turn a canoe sideways in the current, you'll flip it. There is a way things work in the physical realm and we must learn to live with it; reality is one of the great tools of God to grow people up. (And he is *deeply* committed to growing us all up! Don't forget that.) Children learn all the hard ways: the scraped knees, the burnt fingers. Wisdom is largely cultivated on encountering the laws of the physical world and adjusting our lives to accommodate. Better still, we learn to use those laws to our advantage—we cook with that heat; we build with that lumber.

The same holds true in the spiritual realm—there is a way things work. Like the children in a fairy tale, we have been thrust into a collision of *kingdoms*. Kingdoms are realms that are governed by a ruler (the king), and they operate on the basis of *authority*. Back in the story of Daniel and his three-week fast, the angel finally showed up and explained he would have been there sooner but he was blocked by the territorial spirit that held sway over the Persian kingdom. He eventually got through, but did you notice how? He brought in a higher-ranking angel: "The prince of the Persian kingdom resisted me twenty-one days. Then Michael, one of the chief princes, came to help me, because I was detained there with the king of Persia. Now I have come . . ." (Dan. 10:13–14).

The messenger got through the blockade because the mighty archangel Michael came and used his greater authority (and no doubt power). That is what we are doing when we use Jesus' name—we are using his authority. A quick overview might help bring clarity:

God made the earth. He then gave it to Adam and Eve, along with authority to govern it: "The highest heavens belong to the LORD, but the earth he has given to man" (Ps. 115:16). The first man and woman—lord and lady of this earthly kingdom—forfeited their authority through their disobedience. That is how Satan became "the prince of this world" (John 14:30). When the evil one slithered up to Jesus in the wilderness and tried to tempt him out of the cross, he offered him the kingdoms of this world, as if they were his to give: "The devil led him up to a high place and showed him in an instant all the kingdoms of the world. And he said to him, 'I will give you all their authority and splendor, for it has been given to me, and I can give it to anyone I want to. So if you worship me, it will all be yours'" (Luke 4:5–7).

It was his to offer because we turned it over to him at the fall of man. "Prince" of this world means ruler of this world. And he has brought ruin and devastation through his malevolent reign, as Stalin did, as Pol Pot did. When an evil ruler comes into power, it allows evil into the kingdom. A man I knew was in Washington, DC during the inauguration of one of our less respectable presidents of the last century; he said that he could see demons rushing into the White House from all directions. Authority had shifted to darkness.

The epicenter of the tectonic shifts I keep alluding to was the coming of Jesus of Nazareth, Son of the living God—who became the Son of Man—to win it all back. *He won it all back.* Because the abdication of the throne occurred through the sin of Adam, it could only be undone through the atonement for those sins. Through his life of total obedience to the Father, through his perfect atonement for our sins by way of his cross and death, Jesus totally disarmed Satan and all those fallen angels like the Prince of the Persian kingdom: "[God] forgave us all our sins, having canceled the written code, with its regulations, that was against us and that stood opposed to us; he took it away, nailing it to the cross. And having disarmed the powers and authorities, he made a public spectacle of them, triumphing over them by the cross" (Col. 2:13–15).

God the Father, in partnership with God the Son, "disarmed the powers and authorities." The Greek here for "powers and authorities" is *arche* and *exousia*—the exact words Paul used to refer to foul spirits of various rank: "For our struggle is not against flesh and blood, but against the rulers [*arche*], against the authorities [*exousia*], against the powers of this dark world and against the spiritual forces of evil in the heavenly realms" (Eph. 6:12). By the cross our Father and Jesus caught the enemy totally off guard, undermined his claims, disarmed the authority of his stolen throne; the evil one and all his allies have lost their right to hold dominion, and that right has been given to Jesus:

> [Who] humbled himself and became obedient to death—even death on a cross! Therefore God exalted him to the highest place and gave him the name that is above every name, that at the name of Jesus every knee should bow, in heaven and on earth and under the earth, and every tongue confess that Jesus Christ is Lord, to the glory of God the Father. (Phil. 2:8–11)

All of this—the victory, the overthrow of Satan's right to rule, the transfer of authority, power, and dominion to the Son of God—this is what Jesus was referring to when after his resurrection he said, "All authority in heaven and on earth has been given to me" (Matt. 28:18).

Let that sink in; the relief of it will lift a mighty weight off your shoulders. All authority in the "heavens"—the spiritual realms—and all authority on this planet has been handed over to Jesus Christ! Think of the redemption that can now take place because of that one fact.

"Yes—that is my point," you might say. "I believe Jesus won. So why don't prayers work better than they do? Isn't Satan defeated?" Stay with me now, because this has staggering implications for you and the way you pray. The invasion of the kingdom of God *is something that is still unfolding*, right now, today. Jesus is not merely seated upon a throne somewhere up in the sky:

> Christ has indeed been raised from the dead, the firstfruits of those who have fallen asleep. For since death came through a man, the resurrection of the dead comes also through a man. . . . Then the end will come, when he hands over the kingdom to God the Father after he has destroyed all dominion, authority and power. *For he must reign until* he has put all his enemies under his feet. (1 Cor. 15:20–21, 24–25, emphasis added)

That "until" gives us a very different way of understanding how Jesus is reigning at the current moment (and why world events still seem so chaotic). Are all his enemies under his feet? Clearly not; the verse says not, and the evening news illustrates it. Jesus, Son of God, Lord of angel armies, is "reigning *until*" he has finished what he began. The image that comes to mind is the terrible battle for the South Pacific in World War II. Island by island, bunker by bunker, tunnel by tunnel, a bloody battle had to be waged until the enemy was thoroughly and completely rooted out. Yes—we took the beach at Iwo Jima, and the airstrip. The enemy was defeated, but still he fought on; subduing the entire island was an unspeakably savage undertaking.

Much as you see in the world today.

Oh yes, Jesus has won. But his kingdom has—*obviously*—not fully come on this earth. Which brings us to the famous model for prayer, held high by the church down through the ages, the "Our Father," the "Lord's Prayer."

We Invoke the Kingdom

> Our Father in heaven,
> hallowed be your name,
> your kingdom come,
> your will be done
> on earth as it is in heaven.
> Give us today our daily bread. (Matt. 6:9–11)

Held high, repeated ritually, but rarely understood. Have you ever wondered why the Lord's Prayer begins with us praying, "Your kingdom come . . ."? The man who knew best how to pray is telling us to invoke his kingdom. We are, after all, partners in this mission. And this is what he wants us to begin prayer with. The obvious implication is that his kingdom is *not* always come, his will is not always done on earth as it is done in heaven—or what a ridiculous thing to tell us to pray. Why would Jesus urge us to pray for something that has no meaning? He does not tell us to pray that the sun rises tomorrow; we are never urged to pray that the sun will rise again each day. God's will is going to be done, every sunrise. You can rest on that one; nothing to pray about there.

But you *are* told to invoke his kingdom, from heaven to earth.

"Maybe he's referring to his second coming—you know, the return of Christ and his kingdom then." I think this is actually the vague idea in most people's minds when they pray the Lord's Prayer. But the next line goes, "Give us *this day* our daily bread." Today—the prayer is talking about today. "Forgive us our debts . . . deliver us from temptation" are current needs; they will not be needs when we are in heaven. The famous prayer is focused on this moment and our immediate needs. Apparently, our greatest need is for his kingdom to invade our lives and our worlds.

Remember now:

God is growing us up.

In the midst of war.

Prayer is partnership with God.

We are allies with him in the invasion of his kingdom.

It makes perfect sense for Jesus to teach us to invoke his kingdom in our prayers; it makes all the sense in the world.

And opens up staggering opportunities for prayer.

Because one of the most crippling convictions held by believers today is the idea that everything that happens is the will of God. It is a poisonous belief that will destroy your confidence in God; you will end up believing terrible things about him. The news report about a pack of teenage boys who repeatedly raped a little girl with Down syndrome. *That is the will of God???*

Listen very carefully. The Bible makes it perfectly clear that God never causes anyone to sin:

When tempted, no one should say, "God is tempting me." For God cannot be tempted by evil, nor does he tempt anyone;

but each one is tempted when, by his own evil desire, he is dragged away and enticed. Then, after desire has conceived, it gives birth to sin; and sin, when it is full-grown, gives birth to death. Don't be deceived, my dear brothers. (James 1:13–16)

God does not tempt, nor does he cause you to sin. But people sin every day, and their sins have devastating consequences. So there are all kinds of events happening every day that are not *caused* by God. Remember, we live in a world where God has granted to human beings and to angels the dignity of causation, the dignity of making things happen. You get to make things happen, just as God does. God did not cause Adam and Eve to sin, nor did he prevent them from doing so. And their sin had staggering consequences.

I simply want to point out that the defining question in any of those "sovereignty of God" debates is, "Do people make meaningful choices?" Yes or no? If you say yes, then not everything that happens is the will of God. If you say no, then God is the ultimate micromanager and we are all figures in his video game. He caused those boys to rape that precious little girl; he caused ISIS to execute those children. They were carrying out the will of God. Do you see how important this is?

Do people make meaningful choices? Indeed they do. The Scriptures are full of provocations to choose, like when Joshua said to the people of Israel, "Choose for yourselves this day whom you will serve, whether the gods your forefathers served beyond the River, or the gods of the Amorites, in whose land you are living. But as for me and my household, we will serve the LORD" (Josh. 24:15).

What a ridiculous thing to put before them if people don't

really choose. All other commands are utter nonsense as well. So much turns on this—do people make meaningful choices? And the next question you want to ask is, *how* meaningful?

Nicholas Wolterstorff wrote a beautiful and heartbreaking book when he lost his twenty-one-year-old son in a mountaineering accident. *Lament for a Son* is the recorded struggle of a father wrestling with questions like, "Why doesn't God intervene?" and, "What kind of world do we have here?" Speaking of his son, and his mountaineering, Wolterstorff said,

> Why did he climb at all? What was it about the mountains that drew him? I suspect that only those who themselves climb can really know . . .
>
> He was lured by the exhilaration of meeting head-on the intellectual and physical challenge of climbing. Beauty pure from the hand of God, untouched by human hand. And deepest, perhaps, climbing was for him a spiritual experience . . .
>
> To us, soft, small, fragile, unsurefooted creatures scrambling over them, the mountains are menacingly indifferent. How insipid it would be if every misstep, every slip of the hand meant no more than a five-foot drop into an Alpine meadow. The menace is essential to the exhilaration of achievement."[1]

How insipid it would be if God turned every misstep of our lives into a soft landing on marshmallows. And clearly he does not. So we are back to the idea of growing up. When our boys were young, we *did* choose what color socks they wore; when they were very, very young, we even dictated what they put in their mouths. But as they grew older, things changed. They were given more responsibility. One day we handed them the keys to the car. We handed over to them the potential to kill someone, to kill themselves. Maturity sets the stage for more and more meaningful choices.

As William James said, "Our present life feels like a real fight as if there were something really wild in the universe which we are needed to redeem."[2]

Sharing His Authority

Which brings us around to praying "in Jesus' name." We were talking about the overthrow of the kingdom of darkness, and the authority given to Jesus Christ; we were following the actions of Jesus in the world today, reigning *until* he has finished vanquishing evil. The Lord of angel armies—and all his forces angelic and human—are now in the throes of bringing his enemies under his feet, beach by beach, tunnel by tunnel. I believe part of the reason God has left it to be done in this way is because he is growing us up; we too must learn to rule and reign.

In 1 Kings 18 God intended to end the drought, but Elijah had a major role; it was up to his prayers to call down the deluge. As C. S. Lewis said, "He seems to do nothing of Himself which He can possibly delegate to His creatures. He commands us to do slowly and blunderingly what He could do perfectly and in the twinkling of an eye. Creation seems to be delegation through and through."[3] The delegation not only of major tasks but also of the authority to get them done.

Having cast down the usurped ruler of this world, all authority was given to Jesus. And then—trumpets ought to ring out and banners unfurled—he in turn gives his majestic authority to us:

"I have given you authority . . . to overcome all the power of the enemy" (Luke 10:19).

Paul was so excited about this, he prayed earnestly that God would give each of us a personal revelation, in our heart of hearts, on how magnificent it is:

> I pray also that the eyes of your heart may be enlightened in order that you may know the hope to which he has called you, the riches of his glorious inheritance in the saints, and his incomparably great power for us who believe. That power is like the working of his mighty strength, which he exerted in Christ when he raised him from the dead and seated him at his right hand in the heavenly realms, far above all rule and authority, power and dominion, and every title that can be given, not only in the present age but also in the one to come. And God placed all things under his feet and appointed him to be head over everything for the church, which is his body, the fullness of him who fills everything in every way. (Eph. 1:18–23)

God placed all things under the feet of Jesus and appointed him to be head of everything for *who?* For the church—for you and me. And then, to make it perfectly clear, our Father seats us with Christ right there in authority, at his right hand:

> But because of his great love for us, God, who is rich in mercy, made us alive with Christ even when we were dead in transgressions—it is by grace you have been saved. And God raised us up with Christ and seated us with him in the heavenly realms in Christ Jesus. (Eph. 2:4–6)

Talk about lavish and scandalous—you have been given a share in the authority of Jesus Christ, Son of the living God, Lord of the heavens and the earth. Do you wield it in prayer? Can you see that it just might make a difference if you did? Maybe we should pray like Paul, and ask for a personal revelation on the truth of this:

> Father, Jesus, Holy Spirit—I ask you to open the eyes of my
> heart and grant to me a personal revelation on the truth of
> the authority given to Jesus, and how I really do share in that
> authority. Break this through to me.

Oh, friends—we are so far from the pathetic cries of the orphan and slave. We are God's sons and daughters, his friends and allies, now princes and princesses in his kingdom, wielding his authority; and we get to play a dramatic role in the story. When Ananias carried out his orders and restored Saul's sight, he felt free to employ Jesus' name. He acted in the name of the King. So did Peter and John:

> One day Peter and John were going up to the temple at
> the time of prayer—at three in the afternoon. Now a man
> crippled from birth was being carried to the temple gate called
> Beautiful, where he was put every day to beg from those going
> into the temple courts. When he saw Peter and John about to
> enter, he asked them for money. Peter looked straight at him,
> as did John. Then Peter said, "Look at us!" So the man gave
> them his attention, expecting to get something from them.
> Then Peter said, "Silver or gold I do not have, but what
> I have I give you. In the name of Jesus Christ of Nazareth,

walk." Taking him by the right hand, he helped him up, and instantly the man's feet and ankles became strong. He jumped to his feet and began to walk. Then he went with them into the temple courts, walking and jumping, and praising God. (Acts 3:1–8)

Like the centurion, these guys understood authority, and look what happened when they began to exercise it! They didn't call a prayer meeting and ask God to heal the man. *They* did it, in his name. They acted like sons of the King.

Which adds a whole new dimension to understanding just who you are when you pray.

You are not the orphaned child, sitting out in the hall hoping your busy Father will see one of the notes you have pushed under his door; you are not a homeless beggar, standing on the corner hoping God will pass by and hand you a couple of bucks; you are not a refugee, standing in line at the embassy, hoping the Ambassador will hear your request. Not even a faithful servant, humbly trying to do your best.

You are a son or daughter of the living God, a friend and ally, wielding his authority to get things done. And by the way—your eternal destiny is to reign:

In my vision at night I looked, and there before me was one like a son of man, coming with the clouds of heaven. He approached the Ancient of Days and was led into his presence. He was given authority, glory and sovereign power; all peoples, nations and men of every language worshiped him. His dominion is an everlasting dominion that will not pass away, and his kingdom is one that will never be destroyed . . .

But the saints of the Most High will receive the kingdom and will possess it forever—yes, for ever and ever. (Dan. 7:13–14, 18)

Then the King will say to those on his right, "Come, you who are blessed by my Father; take your inheritance, the kingdom prepared for you since the creation of the world." (Matt. 25:34)

With your blood you purchased men for God from every tribe and language and people and nation. You have made them to be a kingdom and priests to serve our God, and they will reign on the earth. (Rev. 5:9–10)

You will reign, dear ones, over glorious kingdoms and realms within the great and glorious kingdom of our Father—a role we certainly need some preparation for. In another favorite Narnia story, *The Horse and His Boy*, the lost prince of Archenland is returned to his father—an orphaned boy, returned to his rightful role, just as we are. But he has some learning to do, some catching up to do before he can assume full responsibility. Shasta, now proclaimed prince, laments to his two horse companions: "It's far worse for me than for you. I am going to be *educated*. I shall be learning reading and writing and heraldry and dancing and history and music while you'll be galloping and rolling on the hills of Narnia."[4]

A prince totally unaccustomed to the ways of the kingdom cannot be entrusted with the throne until he has had some preparation—just as we need *"educating."* We really thought this life was simply about getting a nice little situation going for ourselves and living out the length of our days in happiness. I'm sorry to take that from you, but you and I shall soon be inheriting kingdoms, and we are almost illiterate when it comes to ruling. So God must prepare us to reign. How does he do this? In exactly the same way he grows us up—he puts us in situations that require us to pray and to learn how to use the authority that has been given to us. How else could it possibly happen?

Now we are ready for the Prayer of Intervention.

Six

THE PRAYER OF
INTERVENTION

Just about everything I have covered thus far can be summed up
in a powerful illustration, through a story of both tragedy and
triumph. Jesus spent three years training his apprentices in the
ways of the kingdom. He ascended to the throne so that the Holy
Spirit could come. (For when Jesus was here in body, walking
the dusty roads of Israel, he could only be present to those in his
physical presence. Now that the Holy Spirit has come, Jesus can
be with each of us, personally, intimately, "always, to the very end
of the age" [Matt. 28:20].)

This story picks up after those events—after his ascension, and Pentecost. The young church is exploding; tensions in
Jerusalem are heating to the boiling point. The collision of kingdoms is about to shift from Jesus to his followers. Let's see how
well the young church has learned their lessons on prayer:

About that time King Herod Agrippa began to persecute some believers in the church. He had the apostle James (John's brother) killed with a sword. When Herod saw how much this pleased the Jewish leaders, he arrested Peter during the Passover celebration and imprisoned him, placing him under the guard of four squads of four soldiers each. Herod's intention was to bring Peter out for public trial after the Passover. But while Peter was in prison, the church prayed very earnestly for him.

The night before Peter was to be placed on trial, he was asleep, chained between two soldiers, with others standing guard at the prison gate. Suddenly, there was a bright light in the cell, and an angel of the Lord stood before Peter. The angel tapped him on the side to awaken him and said, "Quick! Get up!" And the chains fell off his wrists. Then the angel told him, "Get dressed and put on your sandals." And he did. "Now put on your coat and follow me," the angel ordered.

So Peter left the cell, following the angel. But all the time he thought it was a vision. He didn't realize it was really happening. They passed the first and second guard posts and came to the iron gate to the street, and this opened to them all by itself. So they passed through and started walking down the street, and then the angel suddenly left him.

Peter finally realized what had happened. "It's really true!" he said to himself. "The Lord has sent his angel and saved me from Herod and from what the Jews were hoping to do to me!"

After a little thought, he went to the home of Mary, the mother of John Mark, where many were gathered for prayer. He knocked at the door in the gate, and a servant girl named

Rhoda came to open it. When she recognized Peter's voice, she was so overjoyed that, instead of opening the door, she ran back inside and told everyone, "Peter is standing at the door!"

"You're out of your mind," they said. When she insisted, they decided, "It must be his angel."

Meanwhile, Peter continued knocking. When they finally went out and opened the door, they were amazed. He motioned for them to quiet down and told them what had happened and how the Lord had led him out of jail. "Tell James and the other brothers what happened," he said. And then he went to another place. (Acts 12:1–17 NLT)

Everything about these events is told so well, in such realistic detail, it must be for our benefit. First, notice how the fates of James and Peter are set in contrast, one against the other, in one narrative flow. The story of James's execution is reported in one sentence—quickly, abruptly, like the event itself, like the swift fall of the sword that took his life. A few words, and it is over; it is so abrupt it is almost violent, as was what happened. Peter's story takes longer to tell, because Peter's story is a story of rescue.

The next thing we notice is that Peter's deliverance appears connected to verse 5: "the church prayed very earnestly for him." Scripture includes and omits things for a reason. James seems to have been seized and executed rather suddenly; the church is not reported to have been praying for him. Were they caught off guard? Then Peter is seized, and the church is reported to be praying earnestly, and his outcome is different. Whatever you want to make of the contrast (they are contrasted with each other), Peter's story clearly illustrates the Prayer of Intervention.

The Greek for "very earnestly" is the word *ektenos*. It is the very same adjective used to describe the prayer of Jesus in Gethsemane: "And being in anguish, he prayed more earnestly, and his sweat was like drops of blood falling to the ground" (Luke 22:44).

What a noble, and sober, comparison. There in the midnight olive grove was held the greatest prayer vigil of all time; we can be sure Jesus was praying with every ounce of his being, empowered by the Spirit, eyes fixed on his Father. That is the comparison being given here for the church's prayers; Eugene Peterson translated the action this way: "the church prayed for him most strenuously" (Acts 12:5 MSG). That is how the church is praying—strenuously—and it produces dramatic results. This is the Prayer of Intervention; they are *intervening* in prayer for Peter, intending to change the outcome of events.

Wouldn't you have loved to have been there with them that night, heard firsthand what, and how, they prayed? Let's see what we can discover from the text.

In verse 5 it mentions they had gathered to pray; then we have the story of Peter in prison, and the appearance of the angel. Did they call down angelic help? Surely these devout Jewish Christians knew Psalm 91 by heart, a great psalm of deliverance: "For he will command his angels concerning you to guard you in all your ways" (v. 11). They knew the famous Old Testament stories of angels coming to the rescue of God's people, stories like Daniel in the lions' den, and his three friends in the furnace. And the writer of Hebrews gave us the worldview of the young church on angelic assistance: "Are not all angels ministering spirits sent to serve those who will inherit salvation?" (Heb. 1:14).

They assumed angels are here to help us, even "serve" us. In a collision of kingdoms, you can be sure they were calling upon all the resources of heaven for Peter's release. It is safe to say they were calling on the angels of God to come and help. Anyhow, an angel does show up.

Notice also that there is quite a bit of story told between the first mention of them praying and Peter's eventual arrival at the house, which takes place later that night. Peter is arrested and thrown in jail; that's when the church is reported to have been praying. He falls asleep—it's doubtful that happened as soon as he was dumped in a cell. Imagine the emotions and adrenaline swirling within him; he knows what happened to James. It was likely hours before he could fall asleep. The angel wakes him up; he gets dressed; he follows the angel through the city streets; the angel disappears; Peter then decides to go to the house where they are praying. The text implies they are still gathered in prayer when he gets there. It is safe to say that their prayers were not quick. They were going at it, apparently for some time—perhaps hours, perhaps all night. Just like Elijah on the mountain (they would also know Elijah's story by heart).

This allows me to interject something about repetition versus the "zap" view of prayer . . .

The Zap View of Prayer

Christians have been told over and over that God is almighty. And indeed he is—the God of four hundred billion billion suns. We have been told he is also sovereign. And indeed he is. Perhaps out of respect, we have adopted the notion that if he is going to act, he is going to act quickly. Bam. Zap. (If we are honest, I think we adopted that perspective because it also relieves us of strenuous prayer.) But is this what we see in so many of these biblical accounts?

Clearly, God does not just zap Peter out of prison. The church has to pray "strenuously" for him; the event goes on into the night. He does not zap the promised rain either—Elijah had to climb to the top of the mountain, and there he prayed eight rounds of intervening prayer. God did send the angel to Daniel the first day he prayed—but it took *three weeks* for him to break through. God didn't just zap Joseph, Mary, and the child Jesus down into safety in Egypt—an angel had to come to them as well; they had to flee in the night.

Even in the great crisis of salvation, with the destiny of human souls hanging over an eternal precipice, even there God does not simply zap. We know his heart longs for man's salvation: "The Lord is not slow in keeping his promise, as some understand slowness. He is patient with you, not wanting anyone to perish, but everyone to come to repentance" (2 Peter 3:9). God desires *every* person to come home to his heart, find refuge in Jesus. He therefore has a gospel message he passionately wants brought to the world. But does he simply reveal salvation to every man, woman, and child in one swift, global, immediate, and irreversible act? Clearly not. Despite his intense desire, he does not zap salvation over the earth. He does the wildest thing ever—he entrusts the task to us. Delegation.

Are you getting the picture? Prayer is not just asking God to do something and waiting for him to zap it.

As those friends, family, and intimate allies of Jesus gathered in the night to intervene for Peter, clearly *they* didn't believe one simple prayer would do it; a few quick "Our Father's" would not have taken all night. Nor would it have been strenuous like Gethsemane.

Intervening prayer often takes time.

And it takes *repetition*, repeatedly intervening and invoking (eight rounds for Elijah).

I was awakened at 3:30 a.m. this morning; at first I did not know why. In our house dark-of-the-night interruptions are usually the result of some spiritual attack, but I did not feel darkness in the room. Gently, the Holy Spirit reminded me that our dear friend is in the hospital in great pain. I turned my heart toward Jesus (I am learning!) and asked him how to pray. As I tuned in to God, I sat up in bed because I knew this needed focus and intention. I then began to call upon the life of God to fill the body of our suffering friend, for that is what I sensed the Spirit urging me to pray:

> Your resurrection life and glory to fill him now, Lord. I
> invoke your resurrection life and glory to fill him now.

Settling into the task, I simply stayed with the invocation:

> Your life, your life, your life . . .

Over and over again, *Your life, your life, your life*. Ten minutes went by, and the Spirit was still moving me to pray. Life was urgently needed at that moment, and I was called upon to invoke it, over and over and over again. Twenty minutes, then thirty minutes of praying, *Your life* . . .

I think many Christians have gotten the idea that repetition is unnecessary, maybe even wrong. Didn't Jesus warn us, "Do not keep on babbling like pagans, for they think they will be heard because of their many words" (Matt. 6:7)? The issue he was addressing was not repetition; the issue was *motive* (he had been teaching all about motive just before he taught this). As two other translations help us see: "Don't babble on and on as people of other religions do. They think their prayers are answered only by repeating their words again and again" (NLT), and, "Techniques for getting what you want from God" (MSG).

Surely when you worship God, you don't simply say, "I love you" and walk away; one sentence is not sufficient for that. If we feared repetition in worship, church services would last three minutes. The Psalms are filled with models of repetition:

> Give thanks to the LORD, for he is good.
>> *His love endures forever.*
> Give thanks to the God of gods.
>> *His love endures forever.*
> Give thanks to the Lord of lords:
>> *His love endures forever.*
> to him who alone does great wonders,
>> *His love endures forever.*
> who by his understanding made the heavens,
>> *His love endures forever.*
> who spread out the earth upon the waters,
>> *His love endures forever.*
> who made the great lights—
>> *His love endures forever.*
> the sun to govern the day,
>> *His love endures forever.*
> the moon and stars to govern the night;
>> *His love endures forever.* (Ps. 136:1–9)

No doubt the people would respond, "His love endures forever" as they worshiped together, repeating it twenty-six times in this psalm! So, repetition is not the issue; *motive* is. As I continued invoking, *Your life*, I wasn't chanting magic spells; it was not the mindless turning of the wooden prayer wheels in a Buddhist temple. The Prayer of Intervention requires sticking with it, as Elijah modeled for us. Effective prayer is often like the felling of a great tree—it takes repeated blows. The church gathered at Mary's certainly knew this because they were at it all night.

We know that Jesus did not mean to teach us to shun repetition in prayer because he used it himself in Gethsemane, praying over and over and over again the same thing: *Take this cup from me.*

An old saint who first taught me to pray—may he be blessed forever—would often say, "When you think you are finished praying, you are probably just getting warmed up."

Often when we first turn to prayer, we are coming in out of the Matrix—that whirling, suffocating Mardi Gras of this world—and it takes us some time to calm down and turn our gaze to Jesus, *fix* our gaze on him. We begin to tune in and align ourselves with God as his partners. That itself takes some time. Much of the early stages of our praying involves not so much interceding but getting ourselves back into alignment with God and his kingdom. Once in that place, we can begin to be aware of what the Spirit is leading us to pray.

Furthermore, as we "press into" prayer, we are not simply begging God to move, but partnering with him in bringing his kingdom to bear on the need at hand. Enforcing that kingdom often requires much "staying with it" and repetition.

Last week I was outside chipping ice off the driveway; winter had fallen like the hammer of Thor, and the ice on our drive had built up enough that we couldn't get our cars up the hill. Unlike soft snow, you can't just shovel ice off. Chipping it away requires a certain technique (there is a way things work); you have to do it in little three- and four-inch sections. In my hurry and impatience, I started trying to take away bigger chunks, but it didn't work. If you stick to small bites with each hit of the shovel, you can "pop" it right off. It's quite satisfying, actually, but it requires patience, a slow and deliberate sticking with it. A perfect metaphor.

This is so important, and hopeful, because many dear folks have given up on prayer, having concluded it doesn't really work, when in fact *quick* prayers often don't work; simple, little prayers aren't sufficient to the needs of this world. There is a way things work.

Back to the Story of Intervention

Back in Acts 12, the church was gathered, and they were praying earnestly, strenuously, like Jesus in Gethsemane. They were praying over time. Notice also that they were praying in unity: "many were gathered for prayer" (v. 12 NLT). Surely they remembered their master's instructions on that: "Again, I tell you that if two of you on earth agree about anything you ask for, it will be done for you by my Father in heaven. For where two or three come together in my name, there am I with them" (Matt. 18:19–20). Prayer is more effective when we can get several people agreeing with us. That's just how it works. This is not to say our personal prayers do not have great power and effect; *they do!* Elijah was alone on the mountain. Daniel appears to have been alone in his fast. Ananias went alone to heal Saul. But let us also accept the truth that the power of agreement in prayer is not to be overlooked.

I think we can also assume the intercessors gathered at Mary's home understood their authority. They sat under Jesus' teaching on it for years; everything that we have covered on authority they had heard and seen demonstrated. In fact, between his resurrection and ascension, Jesus lingered more than a month with his disciples(!). And look what he stayed to give them further instructions on: "After his suffering, he showed himself to these men and gave many convincing proofs that he was alive. He appeared to them over a period of forty days and spoke about the kingdom of God" (Acts 1:3).

He was continuing their education on a theme he had been discipling them in for years. The gospel Jesus taught was not merely the gospel of "salvation." It is repeatedly referred to as the gospel of the kingdom:

Jesus went throughout Galilee, teaching in their synagogues, preaching the good news of the kingdom, and healing every disease and sickness among the people. (Matt. 4:23)

Jesus went through all the towns and villages, teaching in their synagogues, preaching the good news of the kingdom and healing every disease and sickness. (Matt. 9:35)

The kingdom of heaven is like a man who sowed good seed in his field . . . like a mustard seed, which a man took and planted in his field . . . like yeast that a woman took and mixed into a large amount of flour . . . like treasure hidden in a field. (Matt. 13:24, 31, 33, 44)

And this gospel of the kingdom will be preached in the whole world as a testimony to all nations, and then the end will come. (Matt. 24:14)

Jesus had told them to invoke the kingdom; he gave them authority to do so; he also provided instruction on the process:

I will give you the keys of the kingdom of heaven; whatever you bind on earth will be bound in heaven, and whatever you loose on earth will be loosed in heaven. (Matt. 16:19)

He taught them to bind and release. Given all they had seen and heard—given their rich tradition in the Scriptures—I think it is safe to say the prayers on that night at Mary's home might have sounded something like this:

Our glorious Father, Abba, we exalt your name. We glorify you. We worship you tonight. We proclaim your glorious rule, majesty, and dominion. For the sovereign Lord is most high, he reigns over all the nations. You set up kings and pull them down; the nations are yours, O Lord, and you give them to anyone you please. The nations are a drop in the bucket to you. Herod cannot defy the living God. For your kingdom is an everlasting kingdom, and of your rule there is no end.

Jesus, our dear Jesus, we cry out to you. We declare that all authority in the heavens and all authority on this earth has been given to you, Lord Jesus. All authority in the heavenly realms and all authority on this earth has been given to you and you alone. We proclaim it—you are Lord of the heavens

84

and Lord of the earth, Lord of all creation. You are the King
of kings and Lord of lords; Herod is nothing compared to
your power and majesty.

Holy Spirit, come and fill us with your power; we
wait upon you. Come and fill our prayers with power from
on high.

Lord Jesus, our King and Deliverer, we invoke your
authority and your kingdom over Peter's life. Your kingdom
come, your will be done tonight over Peter's life. We
declare and we proclaim that Peter belongs to the Lord
God Almighty. Herod has no claim on him. Peter has been
purchased, ransomed, and redeemed by the blood of God's
Lamb, by the blood of Jesus of Nazareth. We call down the
kingdom of God over Peter, right now, this night. Send your
angel to free him, Lord; break the rod of his oppressors. You
set captives free, O Lord. We proclaim it: you set the captives
free. With a mighty arm and an outstretched hand you freed
your people from Egypt. Come and free Peter now by your
mighty arm and outstretched hand. Show the wonder of your
great love, you who save by your right hand those who take
refuge in you from their foes. Break the chains that hold him,
Lord; reveal your mighty strength.

Almighty God, ruler of the heavens and earth, you
humbled Pharaoh with your majesty; humble Herod now.
Humble Peter's captors. We invoke the power and majesty of
your kingdom over his life tonight, to break every chain that
holds him.

Holy Spirit, we pray you would comfort Peter. Come
upon him now in your love; comfort him, sustain him in his
affliction. Strengthen his faith, O Lord, fill him with hope in

your deliverance. For you are a mighty deliverer. Break the chains that hold him. Send angels to deliver him.

We bind Satan from taking Peter's life. The prince of this world has been cast down; he has been judged. We bind the strong man who has laid this claim upon Peter; we cut him off by the blood of the Lamb, by the blood of Jesus of Nazareth. We bind Satan from Peter now, in the authority of Jesus Christ the Lord. By the blood of the Lamb of God we break every claim upon Peter, and we release the kingdom of God over his life. We proclaim Peter's freedom and we proclaim his release.

"In my distress I called upon the Lord; he reached down from on high and took hold of me; he drew me out of deep waters. He rescued me from my powerful enemy, from my foes who were too strong for me. He brought me out into a spacious place; he rescued me because he delighted in me." Sovereign Lord, our Redeemer, we call to you in our distress. Reach down from on high and deliver Peter; rescue him from his enemies; bring him out into a spacious place. We enforce the majesty of your kingdom and your mighty rule over Peter's fate; we enforce the claims of your kingdom over his life in the authority of Jesus Christ the Lord.

No doubt they kept circling back through each theme, each person adding something to the growing momentum as the Spirit moved them. They were proclaiming the truth, invoking the kingdom, enforcing the kingdom. The Prayer of Intervention involves a flow of "proclaiming, invoking, and enforcing." They proclaimed, they invoked, they enforced, just as the psalms taught them to do—just as Jesus taught them to do.

The last part of the story is just so very human it adds humor and believability to the whole account. Peter miraculously appears at the door, and they are so astounded they don't believe it's him—even though they've been praying all night for this very thing. Don't you appreciate that? You are watching very real human beings here. I'm embarrassed how many times I have been surprised by the answer to a prayer I have been diligently seeking. I love that the Holy Spirit—having just given us a very sober story on the Prayer of Intervention—adds a comic touch at the end.

Then Peter takes off for points unknown, to lay low for a while. These men and women do not have a naïve view of the story they are in. They know they are sheep among wolves.

A Few More Examples

Now we can come back to the wildfire, the angel, and the prayers that saved our home. (It might help you to know that I recently learned from a local pastor that his home was also miraculously spared; ours was not an isolated incident.) The fire jumped its lines and moved with such speed, it took many people by surprise. Like with the account of the execution of James, it may well be that the praying church had not been alerted in time before the fire started devouring homes. Once they saw what was at stake, the strenuous prayer kicked in.

I personally know many of the men and women who were praying for us. Like the crowd gathered at Mary's home, they are people who are trained in the ways of the kingdom; these men and women . . .

- know who they are in the kingdom of God—not orphans, nor slaves, but sons and daughters of the King, his friends and allies;
- believe that intervening prayer is more than just asking God to do something;
- understand authority—and the authority they have been given, and they are bold enough to use it;
- choose to unite with others in prayer in order to increase their effectiveness; and
- accept the truth that the authority they have been given extends over creation.

Jesus made it abundantly clear that his authority extended over the laws of the physical world. He shut down a storm on the Sea of Galilee with a command. He fed five thousand with a few morsels. All of the healings demonstrated his power over creation. As our friends intervened in prayer, one of the things they did was to bring the kingdom of God over our property, enforcing and commanding with authority that the fire "stand down"; they forbid it to cross our property line. And it did not.

When our van was spinning out of control across that field of hailstones, and I shouted, "Jesus!" as I braced for what was about to happen next, it was more than just a Cry of the Heart. It was that, for sure. The Prayer of Intervention does not do away with the Cry of the Heart. But something powerful, forceful, and commanding rose up in my spirit. "Jesus!" was not only a cry for help; it was at the same time a command. A one-word order that meant, "In the name of Jesus Christ, *no!*" I was exercising authority; I was enforcing the kingdom over our immediate need.

We do not have to be passive victims of life, waiting until a distant God chooses to do something. We are friends and allies of our intimate God; he has given us power and authority to change the course of events ourselves. Human beings are meant to intervene, to engage, to make a difference. We *can* move mountains. It's in our DNA.

If you will pray like this, you will begin to see far greater results.

Seven

REMOVING ONE MORE OBSTACLE

I think by this point in our education we are safe to go ahead and dismantle a cherished misunderstanding about prayer. I have been with a number of dear saints—praying saints—who rely on the famous expression, "Prayer moves the hand of God." They built a worldview around it—one of those popular religious sayings that became sacred because it packages a reverent humility in a memorable cliché.

Yet it is heinous—a heinous view of God *and* a heinous view of prayer.

Follow the logic. Prayer moves the hand of God—in other words, God is waiting to move until I pray. That thought alone reflects such a debased view of God I give thanks it is false, foul heresy. The entire story of God toward us begins with God making the first move: "In the beginning God . . ." (Gen. 1:1). That theme carries on throughout the Bible:

You see, at just the right time, when we were still powerless, Christ died for the ungodly. . . . God demonstrates his own love for us in this: While we were still sinners, Christ died for us. (Rom. 5:6, 8)

You did not choose me, but I chose you. (John 15:16)

No one can come to me unless the Father who sent me draws him. (John 6:44)

In the same way, the Spirit helps us in our weakness. We do not know what we ought to pray for, but the Spirit himself intercedes for us with groans that words cannot express. (Rom. 8:26)

The tender, beautiful revelation in the parable of the lost son is that the father could not have seen his son coming from "a long ways off" unless *he* was first looking for his son.

"Prayer moves the hand of God" has poisoned many dear souls. Simply apply this idea to any half-rate earthly father and you will see how vile it is: A little girl of five or six years old is dying of hunger; her father is seated in the next room before a banquet table overflowing with food. But, he will not move to help his child until she *asks?* What kind of father is this? What if she is too weak to ask—will he not move because she does not cry out for his love and help? What kind of man is this?

The girl approaches the door to the banquet hall in as humble and reverent a posture as she can sum up, but she hears nothing in return. Getting down on her knees she tries again, with added tears. Her father remains silent and motionless. What is she to conclude? The same thing most Christians have come to conclude about prayer: "I must not be asking in the right way," or "He doesn't care to move regardless of how earnestly I ask him," or "I guess it isn't his will to help me."

Do you see how putrid the whole foundation is?

In any earthly home we would call this child abuse and thank God the man would not only lose custody of the child but also be thrown in jail. Yet this is our reverent view of *God*? Jesus assures us that his Father is always at work on our behalf: "My Father is always at his work to this very day, and I, too, am working" (John 5:17). I love the way C. S. Lewis described this in *The Silver Chair*. Jill is about to receive the task to find the lost prince. But she is confused because Aslan seems to be assuming she and Eustace ("Scrubb") have come at his call:

> "I was wondering—I mean—could there be some mistake? Because nobody called me and Scrubb, you know. It was we who asked to come here. Scrubb said we were to call to—to Somebody—it was a name I wouldn't know—and perhaps the Somebody would let us in. And we did, and then we found the door open."
>
> "You would not have called to me unless I had been calling to you," said the Lion.[1]

Yes, yes, yes—God wants us to ask. He loves it when we ask. He warns that in some situations, "You do not have, because you do not ask" (James 4:2). God yearns for us to turn to him, seek him. Of course, he uses trial and tribulation to cause us to seek him with all our hearts.

And yes, yes, yes—God does sometimes seem to "wait" to

move until we ask. Any good parent knows this. I have many resources to help my sons (and daughters, now!). But for several reasons I often wait until they ask. Quite often they are not ready to receive my help until they have exhausted their own resources. Often there are vital lessons for them to learn, and if I stepped in prematurely, they would be robbed of those precious lessons. I hope you see the parallels in our lives with God. There is also the beauty of humility that he is cultivating in the human heart; it takes humility to ask.

So *yes*—there are beautiful forms and expressions of prayer asking God to move on our behalf. I oftentimes pray that way too. But this is not the same as the orphan's cry, nor does it imply that God never moves until we get him to. In fact, this was the very lie Jesus was addressing in the parable of the persistent widow.

> Then Jesus told his disciples a parable to show them that they should always pray and not give up. He said: "In a certain town there was a judge who neither feared God nor cared about men. And there was a widow in that town who kept coming to him with the plea, 'Grant me justice against my adversary.'
>
> "For some time he refused. But finally he said to himself, 'Even though I don't fear God or care about men, yet because this widow keeps bothering me, I will see that she gets justice, so that she won't eventually wear me out with her coming!'"
>
> And the Lord said, "Listen to what the unjust judge says. And will not God bring about justice for his chosen ones, who cry out to him day and night? Will he keep putting them off? I tell you, he will see that they get justice, and quickly." (Luke 18:1–8)

Surely you understand that Jesus was *not* characterizing God like that judge. God is not someone you have to beg and beg in order to irritate enough to move his hand. Jesus says so at the end of the lesson. He taught us to call upon him as Father, Abba, Papa. The story is introduced as "a parable to show them that they should always pray and not give up." It is about *persistence*. It is about the Prayer of Intervention. It has nothing whatsoever to do with "praying to move the hand of God." As George MacDonald said,

> It is a comfort [Jesus] recognizes difficulty in the matter—sees that we need encouragement to go on praying, that it looks as if we were not heard, that it is no wonder we should be ready to faint and leave off. . . . Actual delay on the part of God, we know from what follows, he does not allow; the more plain is that he recognizes how the thing must look to those whom he would have go on praying. Here as elsewhere he teaches us that we must not go by the look of things, but by the reality behind the look . . . God hears at once, and will avenge speedily.[2]

"Pounding on the doors of heaven" is the latest version of "prayer moves the hand of God," and one I'm hearing often. "I'm pounding on the doors of heaven," a friend said recently. "I'm not giving up till God moves." They are in serious need, and they are going for it. That's good; that's really good. But they are laboring under a horrible idea: that God is waiting for them to ask enough times, or ask with enough sincerity, or faith, or whatever, to get him to move. Heinous. Any half-rate father would do better for his son. God is not a reluctant participant in your life, bothered by your requests, unwilling to act until he gets tired of hearing the sound of your voice.

We know who he is and who we are. We know what is going on in the world. We understand the invasion, and that we are partners with God invoking the kingdom. We know prayer is not begging God, nor is it merely zap. So, let us kill this religious deception with an axe and bury it forever. It was not given to us by Jesus.

Eight

CONSECRATION— BRINGING THINGS UNDER THE RULE OF JESUS

The Vietnam War still lingers like a dark cloud in the back of the American consciousness. It was harrowing; it was unclear; it was unresolved. The book *We Were Soldiers Once . . . and Young*, and the movie based on it (*We Were Soldiers*), tells the bloody story of the first major battles for US soldiers in the war. On the morning of November 14, 1965, eight Bell "Huey" helicopters dropped the first wave of soldiers into the Ia Drang valley; when those sixty boys hit the ground, they had no idea where the enemy was located, in what strength, or numbers. The scene in the movie shows sixty men spilling out of the choppers and immediately opening fire; a chaos of battle erupts as they unload thousands of rounds of M16 ammo into the tall grasses and trees around them.

Only—the enemy was not there. Not yet. The firing was

entirely one-sided, an outburst of panic. When Hal Moore gets them to stop firing, the valley is silent.

I do not fault those boys for firing at every blade of grass that moved in their first few moments of war; I'm certain I would have started shooting before I even left the chopper. But the scene is a brilliant depiction of how Christians often pray—frantic, impulsive, chaotic.

Last week Stasi and I were helping some friends consecrate their new home—which is a *very* good idea and something that requires focused intention to do well. But in their enthusiasm they jumped straight into praying for "peace" and "laughter" and all the good things they hoped would fill their home in the years to come. Only, they hadn't first brought their home under their authority, and under the authority of Jesus. The blessings of the kingdom of God cannot flow until we first bring things under the rule and jurisdiction of Jesus Christ.

But in our eagerness to see good happen, Christians often jump straight into praying, without first pausing and aligning ourselves with Jesus—like a trombone player who simply starts playing her part without waiting for the conductor; or an athlete who skips all his normal stretches and warm-ups and tries to hurl himself into the game from a cold start. This might be the number one error made by earnest folk. Remember—*there is a way things work.* We are in a collision of kingdoms, and it takes intentionality to bring things under and into the kingdom of God.

In teaching healing prayer, Agnes Sanford used this wonderfully simple analogy:

> If we try turning on an electric iron and it does not work, we
> look to the wiring of the iron, the cord, or the house. We do

not stand in dismay before the iron and cry, "Oh, electricity, *please* come into my iron and make it work!" We realize that while the whole world is full of that mysterious power we call electricity, only the amount that flows through the wiring of the iron will make the iron work for us.[1]

The act of consecration is "repairing the wiring," the first step before God's protection and provision can flow. It is the fresh act of dedicating yourself—or your home, a relationship, a job, your sexuality, whatever needs God's grace—deliberately and intentionally to Jesus, bringing it fully into his kingdom and under his rule. It seems so obvious, now that we state it, but you would be surprised how often this vital step is overlooked (and then folks wonder why their prayers don't seem to be effective).

When I come into my office to work on this book, I don't start banging away on my keyboard; that would be utterly foolish and, frankly, a bit arrogant. This book is far too important; I want it fully under the inspiration and guidance of the Holy Spirit. Plus, the enemy jams the process any way he can. So first—after my daily prayers—I turn on some worship music, get down on my knees, and worship God in my office; I worship Jesus "over" my office and the book I am writing. Then I pray something like this:

> I consecrate my life again today to the Holy Spirit—I
> consecrate my gifting and my writing; I consecrate this book—
> every word, every paragraph, every page, all of the structure,
> the flow, the stories, the very spirit of it. I consecrate this office
> and my computer. I bring this all under the rule of Jesus
> and under the filling of the Holy Spirit. And I call forth the

creative life rule of Jesus Christ throughout my office today, throughout my gifting and all of my writing, in Jesus' name.*

Trust me—it makes a difference. The Scriptures respect the power of consecration. On that terrible and glorious day when the people of Israel witnessed with their own wide eyes the fire of God come down on Sinai, darkness shot through with lightning covering the mountaintop, the day God presented Moses with those legendary stone tablets—before all that took place, Yahweh gave Moses special instructions for his chosen people:

"I am going to come to you in a dense cloud, so that the people will hear me speaking with you and will always put their trust in you." Then Moses told the LORD what the people had said.

And the LORD said to Moses, "Go to the people and consecrate them today and tomorrow. Have them wash their clothes and be ready by the third day, because on that day the LORD will come down on Mount Sinai in the sight of all the people. (Ex. 19:9–11)

Precisely the same instructions are given again, the day before the tribes of Israel were to cross the Jordan and begin the conquest of the promised land (which, don't forget, is a metaphor for entering into all that God has for you). Joshua went through the camp and gave the people the first step essential to their success:

---

* To clarify, I have already prayed the Daily Prayer I will talk about in the next chapter; I don't pretend that this prayer is sufficient. By "the creative life rule of Jesus," I mean that power that was in operation at creation. After all, the world was made through Jesus by the creative powers of God (John 1:3). I want those powers flowing through me as I write!

"Consecrate yourselves, for tomorrow the LORD will do amazing things among you" (Josh. 3:5).

Amazing things indeed—he held back the waters of the river, just as he did with the ocean, so that six hundred thousand people could stroll across without getting their sandals wet. They saw the mighty fortress-walls of Jericho crumble like a sandcastle, and many other miracles. But first, they consecrated. The theme carries on into the New Testament; God is about to launch the great missionary expeditions of Paul, the invasion of Christianity into the known world:

> Now there were at Antioch, in the church that was there, prophets and teachers: Barnabas, and Simeon who was called Niger, and Lucius of Cyrene, and Manaen who had been brought up with Herod the tetrarch, and Saul. While they were ministering to the Lord and fasting, the Holy Spirit said, "Set apart for Me Barnabas and Saul for the work to which I have called them." Then, when they had fasted and prayed and laid their hands on them, they sent them away. So, being sent out by the Holy Spirit, they went . . . (Acts 13:1–4 NASB)

I love the phrase "So . . . they went." It's such an understatement. These men set in motion a series of events that changed the world. Because they "went" *anointed with the power of God*. Notice the connection: First, they consecrated themselves. Meaning, they dedicated themselves afresh to God; they renounced every way they had wandered from him; they presented their lives, their gifting, and their calling completely to Jesus, to be filled again with his Spirit, to be his and his alone.

Because of the collision of kingdoms, consecration is usually the first act of effective prayer; until this occurs it is hard to see anything else good happen. For example, it is essential in healing prayer, where we are invoking the power of God, his radiant life, into a body in order to overcome sickness and restore health. We first need to make sure the wiring—the channels for the power of God—are clear. Therefore we first consecrate that body, as Romans urges us: "Offer yourselves to God, as those who have been brought from death to life; and offer the parts of your body to him as instruments of righteousness. . . . Offer your bodies as living sacrifices, holy and pleasing to God—this is your spiritual act of worship" (6:13; 12:1).

Before the healing power of God can flow into a body, you have to re-present that body to God; you have to bring it under the loving rule of Jesus once again. Referring to the illustration on electricity, Sanford went on to say, "The same principle is true of the creative energy of God. The whole universe is full of it, but only the amount of it that flows through our beings will work for us."[2] Consecration is healing the "connection," so that God's power can flow into our bodies. So we pray something along these lines:

I present my body to Jesus Christ as a living sacrifice;
I present the members of my body to Jesus Christ as
instruments of righteousness. My body has been bought with
the blood of Jesus Christ and it belongs to him. My body
is a temple of the Holy Spirit. I renounce every way I have
misused and abused my body; I bring all those acts under
the atoning blood of Jesus Christ. I rededicate my body and
all its parts to the loving rule of Jesus Christ; I dedicate and
consecrate my body to him in every way. I ask for the blood
of Christ to cleanse my body and make it holy once more.

Holy Spirit, come and fill your temple now; restore my body under the complete dominion of Jesus Christ.

Quite often we will be very specific with those parts of the body that are needing the healing, as in, "I consecrate my bone marrow and my white blood cells" in the case of leukemia, or, "I consecrate my head and my brain" in the simple case of a headache.

"But I'm a Christian—aren't I always under the rule and protection of Jesus?" Yes . . . and no. I wish it were as simple as, "I gave my life to Christ once, so I am forever and always in an unbroken intimacy with him." But you know from your own experience this isn't so. That's a bit like a man saying, "I told my wife I loved her the day we got married; what more is needed?" Listen carefully to this passage:

> Do not let anyone who delights in false humility and the worship of angels disqualify you for the prize. Such a person goes into great detail about what he has seen, and his unspiritual mind puffs him up with idle notions. He has lost connection with the Head, from whom the whole body, supported and held together by its ligaments and sinews, grows as God causes it to grow. (Col. 2:18–19)

Paul is clearly referring to believers who have lost "connection" with Jesus; they have—for some reason or another—wandered out from under his rule. Perhaps it happened through sin; maybe it was simply the result of sloppy living and neglecting those practices that keep us intimate with God; in this case it appears to be goofy beliefs. Certainly the pressures of this world have an effect on us, and the enemy has a vested interest in separating us from

Christ. I think Jesus saw this coming, knew our vulnerability, the wandering propensities of the human race, and that is why he urged us over and over again to "remain in him."

> Remain in me, and I will remain in you. No branch can bear fruit by itself; it must remain in the vine. Neither can you bear fruit unless you remain in me.
>
> I am the vine; you are the branches. If a man remains in me and I in him, he will bear much fruit; apart from me you can do nothing. . . . If you remain in me and my words remain in you, ask whatever you wish, and it will be given you. This is to my Father's glory, that you bear much fruit, showing yourselves to be my disciples.
>
> As the Father has loved me, so have I loved you. Now remain in my love. If you obey my commands, you will remain in my love, just as I have obeyed my Father's commands and remain in his love. I have told you this so that my joy may be in you and that your joy may be complete. (John 15:4–11)

Now, Jesus wouldn't have urged us to remain *in* him unless it was likely we would wander *out* from him. He never urged us to flap our arms and fly like a bird, for the simple reason that it cannot happen. It can't be done. So if he urged us to remain in him, he did so because he knew we might not. Probably would not.

Let me be clear: This *does not* refer to the eternal security of the believer. The Scriptures assure us time and again that once you belong to God, you can never, ever lose that.

> My sheep listen to my voice; I know them, and they follow me. I give them eternal life, and they shall never perish; no one can

snatch them out of my hand. My Father, who has given them
to me, is greater than all; no one can snatch them out of my
Father's hand. (John 10:27–29)

In fact, Paul addressed the issue quite clearly of those who
wander from Christ and don't live lives worthy of any recogni-
tion; he assures us that though their lives might be a waste, they
themselves will be saved:

> But each one should be careful how he builds. For no one can
> lay any foundation other than the one already laid, which is
> Jesus Christ. If any man builds on this foundation using gold,
> silver, costly stones, wood, hay or straw, his work will be
> shown for what it is, because the Day will bring it to light. It
> will be revealed with fire, and the fire will test the quality of
> each man's work. If what he has built survives, he will receive
> his reward. If it is burned up, he will suffer loss; he himself
> will be saved, but only as one escaping through the flames. (1
> Cor. 3:10–15)

But that is not the kind of life we want to live; we don't want
to come into heaven by the hair of our chinny-chin-chins. We
want fruitfulness; we want breakthrough! Then let us soberly
take note that *in terms of daily practice*, and enjoying the full blessings of God's protection and provision, yes, you can wander. The
vine and branches metaphor is specifically referring to the power
of God flowing through us (the electrical wiring of their day).
We "remain" in him so that just as the branches receive their life
force from the vine, we are in position to receive our life force
from God. *That* is why consecration is so important.

Back to the story of helping our friends consecrate their home. The house in question was about thirty years old. They had been living in it for six months when my friend called to say, "Okay, what is going on? The kids are having nightmares, my wife is having headaches, we're fighting all the time. What is this?" My first question was, "Do you know who you bought the house from?" "Not really. It's this older lady." "You have no idea what went on in that house?" "No, no idea." "It would probably be a good idea to bring the kingdom of God there. It was under someone else's dominion for a long time and you have no idea what they let in. All it takes is their kids listening to heavy metal and that provides a huge invitation for foul spirits to come in and hang out there. You don't know what kind of music their kids listened to, what movies they watched, what their religious beliefs were; you don't know what went on in that house."*

So we went back to what should have been done right away, and we helped them consecrate with a prayer like this:

Father, thank you for the blessing and the provision of this
home. We bring it under our authority now, and under the
authority of Jesus Christ. We take full authority over this
home, in the name of Jesus Christ. The keys to this home
have been given to us—authority has been given to us—
and we take a total and complete authority over this entire
home now, in Jesus' name. We renounce all ungodliness and

---

* Sin is typically the reason things get out from under the protection and provision of God. It was Adam and Eve's sin that gave the evil one dominion over us and over this earth; what followed was the suffering and brokenness that has become our daily reality. That suffering and brokenness is what we are trying to fix through prayer. Therefore our first aim ought to be getting things back under the dominion of God, and the provision of his kingdom.

all sinful activity that has ever taken place in this home. We renounce the sins of all previous owners, renters, guests, even the builder. [For those are the things that give the enemy claim.] We cancel every claim the enemy can make here, by the blood of Jesus Christ. We cleanse this home with the blood of Christ—everything spiritual, everything physical. We consecrate and we dedicate this home to the rule of Jesus Christ, and to the Holy Spirit. We consecrate the appliances, the structure and infrastructure, the water and electricity; we consecrate the physical realm and the spiritual realm; we consecrate the land as well. [Walk through every room; do this very deliberately.] Come, Holy Spirit, come and fill every part of this home with the glory of your kingdom, with love, with peace, with holy rest. Jesus, we ask your angels to cleanse this home now, to establish your kingdom here, to build a shield of protection around it. In the mighty name of Jesus Christ the Lord, we now proclaim this home and land and everything in it the property of the kingdom of God.

This is a condensed version, for we certainly always worship through the house and find it helpful to anoint the doors with oil or with communion wine. Finally, having brought it under the rule of Jesus as thoroughly as we can, only *then* can we pray in the joy and love and peace and all the goodness we want to fill the house. And what a difference it makes!

There are *multitudes* of application for consecration.

We do a mini version of this every time we use a hotel room. (My goodness—you have no idea what has happened in that room over the years!) Every time they step into the pulpits, the ministers of God (whoever they may be, whatever their title) will want to consecrate themselves afresh—their messages, their gifts, and their calling—so that the power of God might flow through them. The artist would want to do the same, as I consecrate myself, my office, my work every time I begin to write. You'll want to consecrate your job, your finances, my goodness—even a vacation. *Especially* vacations, anniversaries, and any opportunity for joy; surely you have discovered by this point that the enemy opposes joy. You want to bring it all under the kingdom of God on a regular basis. When we are having guests over, we will always pause beforehand and give the evening to Jesus, bringing it under his rule and the blessings of the kingdom. Joy is opposed, friends; it doesn't just happen because you hope it will.

Consecration is particularly effective when you can do so at the beginning of any endeavor—the launch of a ministry venture, a business enterprise or partnership, a new school year. Our family always consecrates the New Year and our calendar to Jesus around January 1. Certainly you want to consecrate the beginning of a marriage, and then again at least every anniversary.

Speaking of marriage, in an age of epidemic sexual brokenness and devastation like ours (has there ever been an age like this?), the consecration and healing of our sexuality is urgent. Stasi and I both carried a lot of sexual brokenness into our marriage, and we have received innumerable blessings by regularly consecrating our "marriage bed" and our sexuality to Jesus. Unbelievably, for most folks, the idea has never crossed their minds; they have never even thought to consecrate their sexuality and their sexual intimacy with their spouses to God. But then, that leaves it open to the ravages of sin, this dark world, and the evil one. Whether through abuse or the mishandling of our sexuality in our past (and present), most human beings living on the planet at this moment need profound assistance in the restoration of their sexuality. It begins by bringing our sexuality under the lordship of Jesus Christ so that we might experience the restoration available in his kingdom. I have provided a prayer for sexual consecration and healing in the back of this book, but let me give you a glimpse of what I mean:

> Jesus, I confess here and now that you are my Creator and therefore the creator of my sexuality. I confess that you are also my Savior, that you have ransomed me with your blood and you are therefore the savior of my sexuality. I have been bought with the blood of Jesus Christ; my life and my body belong to God; my sexuality belongs to God. Jesus, I present myself to you now to be made whole and holy in every way, including in my sexuality. You ask us to present our bodies to you as living sacrifices and the parts of our bodies as instruments of righteousness. I do this now. I present my body, my sexuality ["as a man" or "as a woman"] and I present my sexual nature to you.

It is the beginning of a whole new life in your sexuality *and* gender wholeness.

Anywhere and everywhere you want to experience the fullness of God's protection and provision, the life and goodness of the kingdom of God, it will help you to consecrate whatever is in question.

Aligning and Enforcing

Think of consecration as "aligning" and "enforcing"—*aligning* yourself, or the subject in question, with Jesus and all the laws of his kingdom, then *enforcing* his rule and those laws over the matter in question. The first steps, which we have covered already, are mostly the aligning part. But often the enforcing requires a bit more oomph, especially if you are having difficulties there. Which brings me to the power of *proclaiming*.

In Acts 9, when Ananias came to pray over Saul, he proclaimed the Lord's intentions there: "Then Ananias went to the house and entered it. Placing his hands on Saul, he said, 'Brother Saul, the Lord—Jesus, who appeared to you on the road as you were coming here—has sent me so that you may see again and be filled with the Holy Spirit'" (v. 17).

Interesting—we don't see Ananias pray to God for Saul; instead, we see him proclaim God's intentions *over* Saul, and that is sufficient to see them fulfilled. The Scripture is mighty and powerful, and proclaiming it as we consecrate has mighty and powerful effects.

Later in Acts, Paul does the proclaiming, in a pretty wild clash of the kingdoms on the island of Cyprus:

> There they met a Jewish sorcerer and false prophet named Bar-Jesus, who was an attendant of the proconsul, Sergius Paulus. The proconsul, an intelligent man, sent for Barnabas and Saul because he wanted to hear the word of God. But Elymas the sorcerer (for that is what his name means) opposed them and tried to turn the proconsul from the faith. Then Saul, who was also called Paul, filled with the Holy Spirit, looked straight at Elymas and said, "You are a child of the devil and an enemy of everything that is right! You are full of all kinds of deceit and trickery. Will you never stop perverting the right ways of the Lord? Now the hand of the Lord is against you. You are

going to be blind, and for a time you will be unable to see the light of the sun."

Immediately mist and darkness came over him, and he groped about, seeking someone to lead him by the hand. When the proconsul saw what had happened, he believed, for he was amazed at the teaching about the Lord. (13:6–12)

We enforce by proclaiming what is true over the subject at hand. For example, we proclaim our authority over our homes because we do have that authority, and we are requiring all things in the heavens and the earth to recognize and yield to that authority. We are announcing to all kingdoms and powers that the authority of Jesus Christ is now in effect *here*. Proclaiming also causes your own spirit to rise up—or the spirit of the person you are praying for. Everything sort of stands at attention when you begin to proclaim the truth.

> Sing to God, O kingdoms of the earth,
>> sing praise to the Lord, "Selah"
> to him who rides the ancient skies above,
>> who thunders with mighty voice.
> Proclaim the power of God,
>> whose majesty is over Israel,
>> whose power is in the skies. (Ps. 68:32–34)

> They will speak of the glorious splendor of your majesty,
>> and I will meditate on your wonderful works.
> They will tell of the power of your awesome works,
>> and I will proclaim your great deeds. (Ps. 145:5–6)

Proclaiming and enforcing are the heart of what we call the Daily Prayer. It is a choice, each morning, to realign ourselves with God the Father, God the Son, and God the Holy Spirit; it is a choice to once again draw upon all the resources of the work of Christ for us. Those who make it a regular practice report wonderful results. So let's turn there next.

Nine

DAILY PRAYER

Now that you have some understanding of the collision of the kingdoms going on all around you, and the need to be intentional about "remaining" in daily intimacy and union with Jesus, I think you have a better grasp of why some sort of daily prayer is essential. Not a quick, little "Father, help me today" prayer; not even interceding for others. Not as your first move. What we need first is *aligning* prayer—bringing ourselves fully back into alignment with Jesus, taking our place in him and his kingdom, drawing upon his life and the power of his work for us.

Over the past thirty years I have progressed from one form of daily prayer to another. I think you will see something of the progression from children to young men to fathers in the development of my morning prayers. I began many years ago with the morning prayer for grace from *The Book of Common Prayer*:

Lord God, almighty and everlasting Father, you have brought us in safety to this new day: Preserve us with your

mighty power, that we may not fall into sin, nor be overcome
by adversity; and in all we do, direct us to the fulfilling of
your purpose; through Jesus Christ our Lord. *Amen.*[1]

It was helpful, if rather brief. Better than not praying at all,
but hardly the Cry of the Heart or the Prayer of Intervention.
Soon my needs grew and I found this one from Neil Anderson to
be far more effective:

Dear heavenly Father, I honor You as my sovereign Lord. I
acknowledge that You are always present with me. You are the
only all powerful and only wise God. You are kind and loving
in all Your ways. I love You and thank You that I am united
with Christ and spiritually alive in Him. I choose not to love
the world, and I crucify the flesh and all its passions.

I thank You for the life that I now have in Christ, and I
ask You to fill me with Your Holy Spirit that I may live my
life free from sin. I declare my dependence upon You, and I
take my stand against Satan and all his lying ways. I choose
to believe the truth, and I refuse to be discouraged. You are
the God of all hope, and I am confident that You will meet my
needs as I seek to live according to Your Word. I express with
confidence that I can live a responsible life through Christ
who strengthens me. I now take my stand against Satan and
command him and all his evil spirits to depart from me. I put
on the whole armor of God. I submit my body as a living sacrifice and renew my mind by the living Word of God in order
that I may prove that the will of God is good, acceptable and
perfect. I ask these things in the precious name of my Lord and
Savior, Jesus Christ. Amen.[2]

Over time my wife and I needed even more horsepower. We were learning and growing in our appreciation for the full work of Christ—all that his cross accomplished, as well as his resurrection and ascension. We were also encountering more demanding situations and stiffer opposition from the enemy. So we began to develop what has become our Daily Prayer.* It, too, has gone through several iterations.

Now, before you jump in, let me offer another piece of advice an old saint gave me years ago when I was just learning to pray. He told me, "Whenever I realize that I have lost paying attention and switched to just 'saying words,' I go back, and pick it up from there." That one act has proven massively helpful in learning effective prayer. This is not mindless repetition; we must be utterly *present* to it. Remember what E. M. Bounds said: "The entire man must pray. The whole man—life, heart, temper, mind, are all in it . . . it takes a whole heart to do effectual praying."[3] There is a need to keep at it—like chipping away at ice.

I will walk you through why I am praying as I do. The first two paragraphs begin with aligning—very intentionally and deliberately coming back under and into God, in every way, and getting yourself in a position to pray.

My dear Lord Jesus, I come to you now to be restored in
you, renewed in you, to receive your life and your love
and all the grace and mercy I so desperately need this day.
I honor you as my Lord, and I surrender every aspect and
dimension of my life to you. I give you my spirit, soul, and

---

* I saw a model for this prayer in a book some twenty years ago, the name of which is long forgotten. Our prayer has developed so much that I doubt it resembles what I saw except in spirit, but I do want to acknowledge the inspiration.

body, my heart, mind, and will. I cover myself with your blood—my spirit, soul, and body, my heart, mind, and will. I ask your Holy Spirit to restore me in you, renew me in you, and lead me in this time of prayer. In all that I now pray, I stand in total agreement with your Spirit and with all those praying for me by the Spirit of God, and by the Spirit of God alone.*

Now, I will often repeat words and phrases as I go along, adding further intentionality. When I say "I surrender every aspect and dimension of my life to you," I will often add, "utterly, utterly, utterly." For we wander, and we have often given ourselves over to other things, and coming home to God therefore requires some time and focus.

Dearest God—holy and victorious Trinity—you alone are worthy of all my worship, my heart's devotion, all my praise, all my trust, and all the glory of my life. I love you, I worship you, I give myself over to you in my heart's search for life. You alone are Life, and you have become my life. I renounce all other gods, every idol, and I give to you, God, the place in my heart and in my life that you truly deserve. This is all about you, and not about me. You are the Hero of this story, and I belong to you. I ask your forgiveness for my every sin. Search me, know me, and reveal to me where you are

---

* If you are the head of a household, you will want to include them by substituting: In all that I now pray, I include [my wife and/or children, by name]. I cover them with your blood—their spirits, souls, and bodies, their hearts, minds, and wills. I ask your Spirit to restore them in you and include them in all that I now pray, acting as their head. In all that I now pray, I stand in total agreement with your Spirit and with all those praying for me by the Spirit of God and by the Spirit of God alone.

working in my life, and grant to me the grace of your healing and deliverance, and a deep and true repentance.

Next, we begin to relate to each member of the Trinity. God is Father, Son, and Holy Spirit—and you have a relationship with each one in unique ways. You need certain things from the Father, from Jesus, and from the Holy Spirit. This is part of our growing up—not just a generic prayer to God but relating to the Trinity as mature allies relate to one another.

Heavenly Father, thank you for loving me and choosing me before you made the world. You are my true Father—my creator, redeemer, sustainer—and the true end of all things, including my life. I love you, I trust you, I worship you. I give myself over to you, Father, to be one with you as Jesus is one with you. Thank you for proving your love for me by sending Jesus. I receive him and all his life and all his work which you ordained for me. Thank you for including me in Christ, forgiving me my sins, granting me his righteousness, making me complete in him. Thank you for making me alive with Christ, raising me with him, seating me with him at your right hand, establishing me in his authority, and anointing me with your love and your kingdom. I receive it all with thanks and give it total claim to my life—my spirit, soul, and body, my heart, mind, and will.

As I shift to Jesus, I pray intentionally into the cross, the resurrection, and the ascension. God the Father has provided everything you need for your restoration in the work of Christ. So many people wonder why God doesn't come through for them more, when they have not even begun to take advantage of and enforce the massive things he has *already* provided. Your Father included you in each element of the work of Christ (all of it was for you, after all; Jesus didn't need these things; you did). Taking our place in, and receiving the fullness of, his work is vital:

Jesus, thank you for coming to ransom me with your own life. I love you, I worship you, I trust you. I give myself over to you to be one with you in all things. I receive all the work and triumph of your cross, death, blood, and sacrifice for me, through which my every sin is atoned for; I am ransomed and delivered from the kingdom of darkness; transferred to your kingdom; my sin nature is removed and my heart circumcised unto God; and every claim being made against me is canceled and disarmed. I take my place now in your cross and death, dying with you to sin, to my flesh, to this world, to the evil one and his kingdom. I take up the cross and crucify my flesh with all its pride, arrogance, unbelief, and idolatry [and anything else you are currently struggling with]. I put off the old man. Apply to me all the work and triumph in your cross, death, blood, and sacrifice; I receive it with thanks and give it total claim to my spirit, soul, and body, my heart, mind, and will.

Jesus, I also sincerely receive you as my Life, and I receive all the work and triumph in your resurrection, through which you have conquered sin, death, judgment, and the evil one. Death has no power over you, nor does any foul thing. And I have been raised with you to a new life, to live your life—dead to sin and alive to God. I take my place now in your resurrection and in your life, and I give my life to you to live your life. I am saved by your life. I reign in life through your life. I receive your hope, love, joy, and faith; your beauty, goodness, and trueness; your wisdom, power, and strength; your holiness and integrity in all things. Apply to me all the work and triumph in your resurrection—I receive it with thanks, and I give it total claim to my spirit, soul, and body, my heart, mind, and will.

Jesus, I also sincerely receive you as my authority, rule, and dominion, my everlasting victory against Satan and his kingdom, and my ability to bring your kingdom at all times and in every way. I receive all the work and triumph in your ascension, through which Satan has been judged and cast down, and all authority in heaven and on earth has been given to you. All authority in the heavenly realms and all authority on this earth has been given to you, Jesus—and you are worthy to receive all glory and honor, power and dominion, now and forever. I take my place now in your authority and in your throne, through which I have been raised with you to the right hand of the Father and established in your authority. I give myself to you, to reign with you always. Apply to me all the work and triumph in your authority and your throne; I receive it with thanks and I give it total claim to my spirit, soul, and body, my heart, mind, and will.

I have been embracing and entering into the work of Christ in a fresh way; now I begin to enforce it over my life and kingdom. (The entire prayer is "proclaiming, invoking, and enforcing.") Sometimes I will pause and allow Jesus to direct me in specific ways as I bring his triumph against whatever is coming against me or mine:

I now bring* the authority, rule, and dominion of the Lord
Jesus Christ, and the full work of Christ, over my life
today: over my home, my household, my work, over all my
kingdom and domain. I bring the authority of the Lord Jesus
Christ and the full work of Christ against every foul and
unclean spirit coming against me. [You might need to name
them—what has been attacking you?] I cut them off in the
name of the Lord; I bind and banish them from me and from
my kingdom now, in the mighty name of Jesus Christ. I bring
the authority of the Lord Jesus Christ and the full work of
Christ against every foul power and black art. I also bring the
full work of Christ between me and every person, and I allow
only the love of God and only the Spirit of God between us.

Holy Spirit, thank you for coming. I love you, I worship
you, I trust you. I receive all the work and triumph in
Pentecost, through which you have come; you have clothed
me with power from on high; sealed me in Christ; become
my union with the Father and the Son; the Spirit of truth in
me, the life of God in me; my counselor, comforter, strength,
and guide. I honor you as Lord, and I fully give to you every
aspect and dimension of my spirit, soul, and body, my heart,
mind, and will—to be filled with you, to walk in step with
you in all things. Fill me afresh, Holy Spirit. Restore my
union with the Father and the Son. Lead me into all truth,
anoint me for all of my life and walk and calling, and lead me
deeper into Jesus today. I receive you with thanks, and I give
you total claim to my life.

---

* This section will make more sense to you after you read the coming chapter on
"warfare prayer."

Then I will cleanse myself once more and put on the full armor of God. A word on this—the armor of God is not a metaphor. I think most people have a vague notion about it, not realizing that the armor is a real thing. You are actually putting on real combat gear in the spirit realm; it is just as real as God, whom you cannot see. Take it seriously; this is not symbolic, but actual equipment provided for your safety:

Heavenly Father, thank you for granting to me every spiritual blessing in Christ Jesus. I claim the riches in Christ Jesus over my life today. I bring the blood of Christ once more over my spirit, soul, and body, over my heart, mind, and will. I put on the full armor of God: the belt of truth, breastplate of righteousness, shoes of the gospel, helmet of salvation; I take up the shield of faith and sword of the Spirit, and I choose to be strong in the Lord and in the strength of your might, to pray at all times in the Spirit.

You will remember in the Prayer of Intervention how angels came to help Peter. "Are not all angels ministering spirits sent to serve those who will inherit salvation?" (Heb. 1:14). That means you—angels are here to serve and help you. So call upon their help!

Jesus, thank you for your angels. I summon them in the name of Jesus Christ and instruct them to destroy all that is raised against me, to establish your kingdom over me, to guard me day and night. I ask you to send forth your Spirit to raise up prayer and intercession for me. I now call forth the kingdom of God throughout my home, my household, my kingdom and domain, in the authority of the Lord Jesus Christ, giving all glory and honor and thanks to him. In Jesus' name, amen.

Many people have reported tremendous results from praying the Daily Prayer, well, daily. The proof is in the pudding, as the old saying goes. Give it a try for a week or two, and see what happens. I think you'll love the results!*

Nowadays I pray an even more extensive version than the one I just laid out. Those of you in front-lines ministry or in times of great personal trial will find that version remarkably helpful; I will include it at the end of the book so as to keep the flow going here. But again, remember—children, young men, fathers. There is no need to strive; if you find another prayer adequate to your needs, by all means use that. The longer version has a great deal more "enforcing" to it, but you must understand—this is always a joy for me to pray. It is not a burden, but a pleasure, not striving, but deeper communion and joyful reigning with Jesus!

---

* The Daily Prayer, in several forms, along with many of the other prayers in this book—including free audio versions for download—can be found at www.ransomedheart.com.

Ten

PRAY NOW!

I've come to the place where I have had to stop telling people, "I'll pray for you."

I simply know that despite my good intentions—and these promises are almost always spoken with good intent—I know that nine times out of ten I just don't remember to follow through. Not until maybe a week or two later, and then I feel guilty that I forgot. I don't like promising something I probably won't live up to. You know how these stories go: Someone you care about tells you of their pain, need, or struggle, and you respond with, "Oh, I'm so sorry to hear that; I'll pray for you." But then, most of the time, we never do. If all the prayers that were promised were actually prayed, this would be a different world by now.

So instead of promising future prayer, what I try to do nowadays is stop, right there in the moment, and pray. Right then and there. It's funny how many Christians this actually throws off guard. "You mean, right now?" "Yes—absolutely. Let's pray."

In the restaurant, in the car, on the plane, wherever. If it's a text or e-mail request, I'll start praying as I type my response, typing out a prayer for them right then and there. Not only does it help me follow through, but it helps them to agree right along with what I have prayed, and agreement is mighty powerful, as we know.

I'm thinking of St. Patrick, how he would pray through the course of the day as he worked: "Tending flocks was my daily work, and I would pray constantly through the daylight hours. The love of God and the fear of him surrounded me more and more—and faith grew and the spirit was roused, so that in one day I would say as many as a hundred prayers and after dark nearly as many again."[1]

He simply did it right there, in the moment. For the truth is, there is no "later." Now is the time to pray, for now is all we really have.

"Jesus, come into this—we invite you into this" is a great place to start. Whatever the need—guidance, direction, encouragement, healing, protection; the canceled flight, the report from the doctor, the tension in relationship—this is the place to start. Invite Jesus right into the heart of it all, right there, in the moment. "Jesus, come into this—we invite you into this."

We do this often in our meetings at Ransomed Heart. Someone will say, "I think we ought to pray about such-and-such," and I'll reply, "Go for it. Lead us. Right now," and we'll stop what we are doing and pray. Because if we don't, we rarely get back around to it. I don't know how many Christian meetings I've been in—board meetings, elder meetings—when all the time is used *talking* about what needs prayer, and we find we have barely a few minutes left at the end for one quick, little, rushed prayer. It's a brilliant ploy of the enemy—keep God's people talking about it, debating, conjecturing, worrying over it, speculating, so they never really get around to *praying.*

By all means, pray when you have time and space to devote yourself to it, time to truly seek God. But pray now too—because you don't know that you will get to it later.

Eleven

"Let There Be Light"— Prayer for Guidance, Understanding, and Revelation

"All that I have done today has gone amiss. What is to be done now?" These words of Aragorn in the Lord of the Rings trilogy struck me deeply the first time I read them, and they have resonated with me in many re-readings since. The man was charged with leading the "fellowship of the ring," and at this point everything has fallen apart—Frodo and Sam have gone on alone; Boromir was slain by the Uruk-hai; the Orcs have taken the two other hobbits captive and fled for Isengard. Aragorn is now left with a very difficult set of decisions—does he follow the ring-bearer, to whom he pledged his life? Or does he hunt the Uruk-hai in hopes of sparing their little friends unspeakable torment? "Before he died Boromir told me that the Orcs had bound them; he did not think that they were dead. I sent him to follow

Merry and Pippin; but I did not ask him if Frodo or Sam were with him: not until it was too late. All that I have done today has gone amiss. What is to be done now?"¹

What is to be done now? Of all the prayers that rise from human lips on this troubled planet, the vast majority must be some version of, "*Help!*" That's why we began with the Cry of the Heart. But second place of "most often prayed" has to be in the genre of, "God—what am I supposed to *do*?" Guidance, clarity, direction—doesn't that seem to be one of the main reasons we pray at all? *What do we do about our son? Should I take this job? Where should I go to school? What am I supposed to do with my life?*

I am currently seeking God's will on a matter very important to me and to our ministry; it feels weighty, and the implications feel almost ominous. Thus, I am getting stressed out—which then hurts my ability to discern what God is saying to me. Which only increases my desperation to hear, and the whole thing is spinning into a tight, little Gordian knot. I have to pause, back up, and consecrate myself and the matter at hand. I've got to settle things down inside and go about the process *not* like the trombone player playing his own little tune. So I turn to a story from Daniel's life.

Daniel is serving in the court of Nebuchadnezzar, king of Babylon, who has set himself up as "king of kings" and is going to reveal himself time and again as a dangerously impulsive man (the monarch who orders Daniel's friends thrown into a furnace to be burned alive, among other things). He is as self-absorbed as King Lear and as dangerous as Hitler. And at the moment, the tyrant is haunted in the night:

> In the second year of his reign, Nebuchadnezzar had dreams; his mind was troubled and he could not sleep. So the king

summoned the magicians, enchanters, sorcerers and astrologers to tell him what he had dreamed. When they came in and stood before the king, he said to them, "I have had a dream that troubles me and I want to know what it means."

Then the astrologers answered the king in Aramaic, "O king, live forever! Tell your servants the dream, and we will interpret it." (Dan. 2:1–4)

Nebuchadnezzar, "Destroyer of Nations," goes on to set up an impossible scenario—not only does he require his "magicians, enchanters, sorcerers and astrologers" to interpret his dream; he won't even tell them what the dream was. They have to first discover *what* he dreamed, and then tell him what it means. Given the phantasmal world of dreams (I had a long one about a rhinoceros in a swimming pool last night), the options are both limitless and bizarre. Oh, and here's the clincher—the king threatens death by mutilation, and annihilation of their households: "I am serious about this. If you don't tell me what my dream was and what it means, you will be torn limb from limb, and your houses will be demolished into heaps of rubble!" (v. 5 NLT).

In doing so, the pompous, superstitious Machiavelli breaks the first rule of seeking guidance: you must take the pressure off. This is essential. Pressure nearly always guarantees you will have a hard time discerning what God is saying, if you hear anything at all. Pressure clenches up your heart and soul and ties all your insides in rubber-band knots. Even if God is shouting, it is unlikely he can get through to you because of the chaos. Daniel appears to understand this (he is a wise man, after all). His first move is to buy himself some time to go and pray about it—thus calming the situation down—and he asks his friends to join in prayer with him, and for him. Yahweh answers, and here is Daniel's praise:

> Praise be to the name of God for ever and ever;
>> wisdom and power are his.
> He changes times and seasons;
>> he sets up kings and deposes them.
> He gives wisdom to the wise
>> and knowledge to the discerning.
> He reveals deep and hidden things;
>> he knows what lies in darkness,
>> and light dwells with him.
> I thank and praise you, O God of my fathers:
>> You have given me wisdom and power,
> you have made known to me what we asked of you,
>> you have made known to us the dream of the king.
> (2:20–23)

Because this is such a beautiful story of finding God in the midst of enormous pressure for guidance, I will often turn Daniel's praise into a prayer when I am seeking the unraveling of my own mystery:

> O Father, wisdom and power belong to you. You change
> times and seasons; you set up kings and depose them. You
> give wisdom to the wise and knowledge to the discerning.
> You reveal deep and hidden things; you know what lies
> in darkness, and light dwells with you. Father—I ask for
> wisdom and power, I ask you to make known to me the
> answer to this riddle.

If anything, I am proclaiming to my own soul and spirit what is true; I am reminding myself that God can and does reveal mysteries, and that sets me in a far better position to receive what God is saying to me. I will also lean into Paul's prayers for guidance: "For this reason, since the day we heard about you, we have not stopped praying for you and asking God to fill you with the knowledge of his will through all spiritual wisdom and understanding" (Col. 1:9).

I'm introducing a technique I will address more later—praying scripture, especially when we don't know what else to pray. Meanwhile, if this is how the saints of old sought guidance, it gives me confidence to pray along these lines.

> For this reason, ever since I heard about your faith in the Lord Jesus and your love for all the saints, I have not stopped giving thanks for you, remembering you in my prayers. I keep asking that the God of our Lord Jesus Christ, the glorious Father, may give you the Spirit of wisdom and revelation, so that you may know him better. I pray also that the eyes of your heart may be enlightened. (Eph. 1:15–18)

When seeking clarity, we will almost always ask for the Spirit of wisdom and revelation. Both are needed. Sometimes, wisdom holds the answer. Other times, we need a revelation from God (as did Ananias, when the situation seemed to shout, "Don't go near Saul!").

The key to receiving answers to prayers for guidance is to let go of our constant attempt to "figure things out." Really, it is almost incessant; I will be in the midst of seeking the God of four hundred billion billion suns on some issue of guidance, and in the midst of asking him, I am thinking through the options, trying to figure it out as I pray. I've been in hundreds of meetings where Christians gathered to seek God's counsel on some matter, but they spent the entire time trying to figure it out. I must be forthright here: God has some rather strong feelings about those who choose to walk in the light of their own counsel:

> Let him who walks in the dark, who has no light, trust in the name of the LORD and rely on his God. But now, all you who light fires and provide yourselves with flaming torches, go, walk in the light of your fires and of the torches you have set ablaze. This is what you shall receive from my hand: You will lie down in torment. (Isa. 50:10–11)

> Lord, help us; Father, forgive us. Forgive us for trying to figure it out even while we are in the motions of seeking your help. We surrender figuring it out; we would rather have your light and your counsel.

And can I add how fruitless it is to seek God's counsel while you are privately committed to one course of action over all others? We must surrender our agendas. We must surrender our "best thoughts" on the matter. We must surrender our secret desires. When we do this, we are in a much better place to receive God's thoughts on the situation.

Lastly—or more often, firstly—I almost always use the technique of praying, "Let there be light." This is the first command in the Bible (Gen. 1:3). God calls forth light before he creates the sun! Throughout the Old and New Testaments, you see God's people crying out for his light to shine upon them, shine upon their paths:

Send forth your light and your truth,
    let them guide me. (Ps. 43:3)

Your word is a lamp to my feet
    and a light for my path. (Ps. 119:105)

I will lead the blind by ways they have not known,
    along unfamiliar paths I will guide them;
I will turn the darkness into light before them
    and make the rough places smooth.
These are the things I will do;
    I will not forsake them. (Isa. 42:16)

God is the source of all clarity and truth, all wisdom and revelation. His light sheds light on all things. As David proclaimed, "In your light we see light" (Ps. 36:9), or, "You are the fountain of life, the light by which we see" (NLT).

The "light" of God—which preceded actual sunlight—is the luminosity of his presence, his Spirit; it is his radiance. It is an actual thing, not a metaphor. When the angels visited the shepherds on the night of Christ's birth, "the glory of the Lord shone around them" (Luke 2:9), making the night like day. So we will often call upon the light of God when we are trying to sort out a quandary. Just last night, Stasi was not doing well. She seemed low, or down, as though she was under some sort of fog. Rather than just playing our trombones, we paused and began to ask for the light of God to shine over her and over the situation:

Let there be light. We proclaim Genesis 1:3: let there be light. Father, shine your light on this—shine your light over Stasi's life. What is going on here, Lord? We call forth the light of God over this. Let there be light!

After a few minutes of simply praying for light, sure enough, God revealed to us that there were some sources of darkness and oppression that had gotten in (which, when you are under them, you hardly notice yourself; it all feels so true and even normal). Having gotten the "light," we were then clear on what and how to pray, and soon she was feeling better.

How to Pray for Guidance

Let's bring this all together into a way of praying for guidance, clarity, or revelation.

First off, do whatever you can to reduce the pressure. Pressure is a killer; it nearly always gets in the way of hearing from God. As best you can, lay down the pressure as you seek guidance. Drama never helps; stress never helps. Give the search some breathing room. Take a deep breath yourself.

Second, be open to whatever it may be that God has to say to you. If you are, in truth, only open to hearing one answer from God—yes, you should buy *that* house—then it's not likely you will hear anything at all. More sadly, if you do hear a yes, you won't be able to trust it. Surrender is the key. Yield your desires and plans and hunches to the living God so that you might receive from him something far better: his counsel. Consecrate the matter; consecrate the *process* of decision making too!

Third, do not fill in the blanks! Do not spend half your energy trying to figure it out while you are giving the other half to seeking God. You do *not* want to "walk in the light of your own fires!" Far better to live with the uncertainty for a while than to be your own counselor.

Finally, when it comes to major decisions, give it some time. Don't try and get this done in five minutes.

You'll notice that I am suggesting in the following prayer that you pray to the Holy Spirit specifically. The reason is simple: it is the Holy Spirit who was given to us as our Counselor, the one who will lead us into the truth:

> If you love me, you will obey what I command. And I will ask the Father, and he will give you another Counselor to be with you forever—the Spirit of truth. (John 14:15–17)

> But when he, the Spirit of truth, comes, he will guide you into all truth. (John 16:13)

It makes sense, then, that we would seek the Spirit when we are seeking counsel.

> Holy Spirit, I need your help. I come to you in need of your counsel, your guidance and direction. Wisdom and power belong to you, God. You change times and seasons; you set up kings and depose them. You give wisdom to the wise and knowledge to the discerning. You reveal deep and hidden things; you know what lies in darkness, and light dwells with you. Holy Spirit—I ask for wisdom and power, I ask you to make known to me the answer to this riddle.
>
> But first I consecrate my life to you, including all my plans and decisions. I consecrate this decision to you; I

consecrate the process to you as well. I bring all of this under the rule and under the dominion of Jesus Christ, who is Lord.

I surrender all my hopes and dreams, all my desires, and all my fears to you, God. I surrender my hunches, my own thoughts and plans, and I ask you, God, for your clear and true leading in my life. You have promised me, "I will instruct you and teach you in the way you should go; I will counsel you and watch over you" (Ps. 32:8).

I need your counsel, Holy Spirit. Come into this decision-making process. Shine your light here and banish all confusion; deliver me from falsehood and fear, from false directions and foolish choices. I want to know the way you have for me. I also lay down in this moment the pressure to get the answer right; I lay down the pressure to hear from you clearly. I simply ask you to speak to me, God.

Let there be light. We proclaim Genesis 1:3: "Let there be light." Holy Spirit, shine your light on this—shine your light over this decision, over everything involved. What is going on here, Lord? We call forth the light of God over this. Let there be light!

I ask you, God, to fill me with the knowledge of your will through all spiritual wisdom and understanding; I ask you for the Spirit of wisdom and revelation here.

Now get specific. "Do you want me to take this job?" or "Is now the time to move?" If it is a complex decision, try and break it down into parts: "Do you want us to move, Lord? Should we move now, or wait? Do we move in with our folks while we look for a place, or stay here until we have found one?" Complex decisions are better handled in bite-size pieces; the old maxim asking,

"How do you eat an elephant?" is answered with, "One bite at a time." Take it one step at a time.

If you feel you are receiving counsel, guidance, or direction from the Holy Spirit, then ask him to confirm it. Confirmation is important when it comes to big decisions, and it gives you a settled assurance that you are in fact following God's will.

> Holy Spirit, thank you for speaking to me. Now I ask you to confirm your counsel through another source. Speak to me through your Word, through the counsel of others, through events. Bring me confirmation, Lord.

If you haven't heard anything yet, try another round of prayer:

> Holy Spirit, I bring myself under your lordship, under your rule and influence. I consecrate myself to you again. I need your counsel. You promised me that you would instruct me and teach me in the way I should go. Come into this decision-making process. Shine your light here and banish all confusion; deliver me from falsehood and fear, from false directions and foolish choices. I want to know your will in this, whatever it may be. Let there be light; may the light of God shine all over this. Do you want me to [ask a specific question]? Is this your will for me?

If clarity doesn't seem to be coming, then walk away and let it rest for a while. Take up the prayer again tomorrow.

If for some reason you have to make a decision now (Do you *really* have to make the decision now? This can't wait one more day?), then use your best judgment but add this prayer:

Father, I ask you to come into this decision; I pray you would
block my path if I haven't chosen well. Close every door,
thwart every move if this isn't your will for me. Come and
guide me.

We have also found it to be helpful to ask a different question
when we don't seem to be getting any clarity on the one we have
been asking. Quite often God wants to address some other issue
first, and he will be silent on one matter until we let him speak
on the other. (This is more common than you might think, so be
open to asking!)

Holy Spirit—is there something else you want to say to us?
Is there something you want to address before you speak to
this? What should we be focused on right now—what do you
want to speak to? Shine your light on that; make it clear to
us. We surrender the process and we allow you to speak into
whatever it is you want to speak into.

Now, I am making an assumption here: God speaks to us. In
many, many ways. But most often, he wants to speak to us intimately, personally; he wants us to hear his voice and feel confident
that we are hearing from him. The beauty of prayer for guidance
is that it requires two-way communication; we can't just make
prayer speeches at God; we need to hear from him! Which brings
us to listening prayer—we'd better turn there next.

Twelve

LISTENING PRAYER

I could tell our prayers were not working; I'm not exactly sure why, but I just had a strong sense nothing was going to happen. We were praying for a dear friend who seemed to keep getting sick, over and over again. He would get well, then fall back into some illness. It was a cycle that was undermining his faith and ours. So we gathered a group of folks to lay hands on our friend and pray for physical healing. Only, it wasn't working, and I could tell it wouldn't even if we kept at it.

I paused, and quietly in my heart I asked Jesus, *What is going on here, Lord? What are we doing wrong? How do we change the way we are praying?*

Jesus replied, *Ask him how he feels about his body.*

So I interrupted the prayer—an awkward but necessary thing to do—and told our friend, "I think Jesus is asking you a question: How do you feel about your body?" His cynical reply was immediate: "Easy—I hate my body." And there was our answer; there was the break in the wiring. You can't bring blessing into a body while the owner of that body is cursing it! He first needed to break those agreements with self-hatred, specifically hatred of his body, and all the judgments he was bringing against himself. Having done that, we were able to resume prayer and soon he was feeling well again.

Ask God What to Pray

The single most significant decision that has changed my prayer life more than any other, the one step that has brought about greater results than all others combined is this (drum roll, please) . . .

Asking Jesus what I should pray.

So simple, and so revolutionizing! Utterly obvious once we consider it, but something we so rarely practice. That is probably one of the side effects of the "prayer is just asking God to do something" view; no doubt it is also more of the negative consequences of the orphan-and-slave mentality. But if prayer is in fact a partnership, then I want to be in alignment with God! For here is his promise to us: "This is the confidence we have in approaching God: that if we ask anything according to his will, he hears us. And if we know that he hears us—whatever we ask—we know that we have what we asked of him" (1 John 5:14–15).

Breathtaking. More trumpets! This one promise alone is so wonderful, so hopeful; it ought to make our hearts sing, courage and faith swelling within us like a rising volcano. If we pray in line with God's will, we can stand firmly on the promise *it will be done.* Amen will finally become *AMEN!*

"But how do I know what the will of God is?" Now, that is the sixty-thousand-dollar question. Let me assure you that you can; God does not torment us by hiding his will from us, though at times it does take a little effort to discern it. Both Elijah and Ananias were praying with confidence because they clearly heard from God. I believe that confidence can be ours.

Not Just Sympathy

Our little fellowship has grown so much in our understanding of prayer over the past thirty years. (And God has been so kind, every step of the way, honoring the efforts of "children" and "young men" as we moved toward maturity.) We have seen many breakthroughs—physical healings, psychological healings, deliverances, rescued marriages, rescued lives. We've seen the weather change, just as James promised we would (James 5:17–18). Many, many times.

But despite all the stunning victories in our past, I never assume I know what the new prayer need before me requires. If someone asks me, "Pray that my mother and my father reconcile," I don't simply start praying that. For one thing, I do not know with any sort of certainty that reconciliation is what God is doing in this moment. It may well be the will of God that her parents reconcile, but it may also be that *first* he wants to address something in their character. God doesn't just put Band-Aids on things; it would be far more like him to first deal with the sin that was poisoning the marriage, and then bring about reconciliation.

I want to live and pray like God's intimate ally, so I turn my gaze toward God and ask, *What do you want me to pray for her mother and father? Show me what to pray.* Those prayers are far more effective because they are aligned with his will. They are aligned with what he is doing in the situation at this particular moment.

And it is a hard thing to do because the needs that drive us to prayer so often pull on the heartstrings of our deep love and concern for others. As Oswald Chambers warned, we have to be careful we don't simply start praying our sympathies for the person or his need:

> Whenever we step back from our close identification with God's interest and concern for others and step into having emotional sympathy with them, the vital connection with God is gone. We have then put our sympathy and concern for them in the way. . . . It is impossible for us to have living and vital intercession unless we are perfectly and completely sure of God. And the greatest destroyer of that confident relationship to God, so necessary for intercession, is our own personal sympathy and preconceived bias. Identification with God is the key to intercession, and whenever we stop being identified with Him it is because of our sympathy with others, not because of sin.[1]

A difficult word, but we are pressing into maturity both in our own character and in our partnership with God, and Chambers's admonition must not be ignored. Be careful you do not let your sympathies get in the way! Once again, this is far too common. You've been in those prayer sessions, where someone just launches in and starts praying out of her emotional response to the situation; it is often beautiful and well-intentioned, but it is also typically ineffective. Peter is still in jail. There isn't a cloud on the horizon.

Now yes, yes—*of course we pray moved by love and concern.* Of course we do. I began this book with the Cry of the Heart; it holds a treasured place in prayer. But we are now talking about the Prayer of Intervention, and the promise we are banking on is that if we are praying in alignment with what God is doing, we will see results. Like the first disciples, our posture needs to be, "Lord—teach us to pray." Not just in a book or sermon, but right here, now, in the moment; teach me how to pray *about this*.

That is why I am careful how I bring my emotion, or my experience, to the need at hand. I don't ignore them; but neither do I let them *dictate* what I am praying. Our testimonies of previous results are valuable, and they may come into play. But this is a very dynamic story we find ourselves in, and as we mature in prayer, let us be careful not to assume this situation is exactly the same as the one before. You will want to ask God what needs to be prayed.

Prayer is not making speeches to God; it is entering into conversational intimacy with him. Father to son or daughter, friend to friend, partner to partner, essential prayer is conversational. It involves a give-and-take. Remember the playful exchange between Ananias and Jesus? "You want me to do *what*?" "Go to this specific house. Place your hands on him." "Wait a second—really?" I understand that prayer speeches are what most of us have seen modeled, but there is a fabulous intimacy and effectiveness available to us as we pause and let God say something in return.

Our God Yearns to Speak

I tell you the truth, the man who does not enter the sheep pen by the gate, but climbs in by some other way, is a thief and a robber. The man who enters by the gate is the shepherd of his sheep. The watchman opens the gate for him, and the sheep listen to his voice. He calls his own sheep by name and leads them out. When he has brought out all his own, he goes on ahead of them, and his sheep follow him because they know his voice. . . . Whoever enters through me will be saved. He will come in and go out, and find pasture. The thief comes only to steal and kill and destroy; I have come that they may have life, and have it to the full. . . . I have other sheep that are not of this sheep pen. I must bring them also. They too will listen to my voice, and there shall be one flock and one shepherd. . . . My sheep listen to my voice; I know them, and they follow me. (John 10:1–4, 9–10, 16, 27)

Four times in this passage alone Jesus repeats himself, to make it perfectly clear: his sheep hear his voice. We are *meant* to hear the voice of God. This is one of the lost treasures of Christianity—an intimate, conversational relationship with God is available, and is meant to be normal. Here in the gospel of John, Jesus is describing his relationship with us, how he is the Good Shepherd and we are the sheep in his care. He warns us that we live in dangerous country. There are wolves. There are false shepherds. There is a thief who comes to steal, kill, and destroy. The only hope we have to stay safe and find good pasture is to follow our Shepherd closely. Lovingly, tenderly, and yet firmly Jesus is urging us— don't just wander off looking for pasture, looking for the life you seek. Stay close. Listen for his voice. Let him lead.

I realize that many dear followers of Christ have been taught that God only speaks to his sons and daughters through the Bible. The irony of that theology is this: *that's not what the Bible teaches!* The Scriptures are filled with stories of God speaking to his people—intimately, personally. Adam and Eve spoke with

God. As did Abraham, Moses, and Elijah. So did Noah, Gideon, Aaron, Isaiah, Jeremiah, Ananias, and the apostle Paul. On and on the examples go.

> In the course of time, David inquired of the LORD. "Shall I go up to one of the towns of Judah?" he asked.
> The LORD said, "Go up."
> David asked, "Where shall I go?"
> "To Hebron," the LORD answered." (2 Sam. 2:1)

Over and over again, the Scriptures provide doctrine and examples that we are meant to hear God's voice:

> He wakens me morning by morning,
>   wakens my ear to listen like one being taught. (Isa. 50:4)

> Today, if you hear his voice,
>   do not harden your hearts. (Ps. 95:7–8)

> Here I am! I stand at the door and knock. If anyone hears my voice and opens the door, I will come in and eat with him, and he with me. (Rev. 3:20)

I love this passage from Revelation because this is the risen Christ speaking, and he is speaking not to the unbeliever but to his church. His offer is clear—he *is* speaking. If we hear his voice and open the door of our lives to him, Jesus will come closer, become even more intimate with us. For this very intimacy we were created! And it is a rescue, a comfort, a source of a thousand blessings, and it also changes the way we pray as we *ask him* what to pray!

Learning to Listen

The first step in learning to hear the voice of God is to ask simple questions.

I find it nearly impossible to hear when I am caught up in drama, stress, or immense pressure. Including urgent time-pressures, as in, *I have to hear and hear NOW!* That is the spiritual equivalent of saying to yourself as you lie down for bed, *I simply MUST get a good night's sleep tonight!* For you know what happens—the stress itself makes it practically guaranteed you won't sleep. Or hear from God, in the case of listening prayer. Do not try to begin with huge and desperate questions like, "Am I supposed to marry this person?" or, "Do you want me to quit my job tomorrow?" or, "Do I have a brain tumor?" God can and does speak into those questions, but starting there is the equivalent of learning to play the piano by expecting yourself to sit down and play a symphony by Mozart. My goodness—let us be kind to ourselves! I find that to hear the voice of God, I must be in a place of quietness and surrender. Beginning with smaller and simpler questions helps me do that.

We've been tracking along with the story of Elijah. Before his triumphant prayer vigil, which called down the rain that broke the three-year drought, the mighty man of God had the famous showdown with the prophets of Baal, resulting in the execution of every one of them. Elijah *then* called down the rain, and after that we find him . . . running for his life from the evil Jezebel. (Don't you just love the humanity of these characters? It makes the Bible so much more real, and their example so much more accessible to us!) God then spoke to Elijah again:

The LORD said, "Go out and stand on the mountain in the presence of the LORD, for the LORD is about to pass by."

Then a great and powerful wind tore the mountains apart and shattered the rocks before the LORD, but the LORD was not in the wind. After the wind there was an earthquake, but the LORD was not in the earthquake. After the earthquake came a fire, but the LORD was not in the fire. And after the fire came a gentle whisper. (1 Kings 19:11–12)

What a lovely phrase—"a gentle whisper." A "still small voice" as other translations have it. To hear that gentle whisper, we need to calm ourselves down. We quiet our hearts and do our best to shut out all drama. I like to go into a room by myself if I can, or, if I am in my car, I will turn off the radio and let it be my quiet, little sanctuary. I do believe that as we grow in our intimacy with God, our ability to hear his voice grows and we can recognize him speaking in times of great trial. But it is not a good idea to start there or only reach out to hear from him in urgent moments.

Quiet yourself; settle down.

I will then take a simple question to bring before him, something like, "Do you want us to have dinner with the neighbors?" or, "Would you have us reach out to my folks this weekend?" The point being, I choose a matter where there is not a great deal at stake, one where I'm not so personally invested that I fear what God might say. It allows me to sit with the question quietly, with an open heart. As I do, it also helps me to repeat the question to God: "Do you want us to have dinner with the neighbors tonight?" Repeating the question in prayer helps me settle myself before him and stay focused.

To be clear, I am not listening for an audible voice, as I would if you and I were talking. I am listening for his gentle voice *within*, for that is where Jesus dwells—within our very hearts (Eph. 3:17).

And as I do, I am also keeping my heart open to whatever answer he has for me. This is crucial. If I am really only open to hearing yes or no, if I am not really asking God's counsel but have already decided in my mind what I am going to do, then the whole thing is play-acting. Surrender, true open-handedness, on the question before me is crucial to hearing from God.

That is a beautiful part of this whole process of learning to listen, this question of our openness to whatever he has to say to us. This is forming in us unreserved obedience, which deepens our holiness and deepens our intimacy with God. Surrender prepares us to hear; it opens our hearts and our spirits to God. As we bring to him matters in which we *do* have strong personal desires, the choice to lay it all before him and allow him to say anything he wants to us not only enables us to hear but also gives us confidence that in fact we *have* heard from God. If I know I have been perfectly honest before Jesus, and allowed him to say anything at all to me, then when he does say yes to my heart's desire, I can receive that yes and not think I've made it up myself—for I know I was also willing to hear no.

These are the basic steps: Start with small and simple questions, yes or no questions if possible. Quiet yourself; pull away if you can to a quiet place and shut out all other distractions. Repeat the question as you pray and listen—that helps dial you in and keeps you focused. Bring your heart into a place of surrender.

Now, if I am having a hard time hearing God's voice, or being certain that I *have* heard, I will sometimes "try on" one answer, then the other. Still in a posture of quiet listening, I will add to my prayers, "Are you saying yes, Jesus? Are you saying you want us to go?" Pause. Listen. "Or are you saying no—you don't want us to go?" Often as we "try on" one answer or another, our spirit can feel the guidance of the Holy Spirit through a confirmation, or a strong sense of reservation.

One other thing I have found helpful as I cultivate conversational intimacy is to first ask God a question I know the biblical answer to. For example, I will ask him, "Do you love me, Jesus?" because I know the Scriptures have answered that, *yes*, beyond all doubt he does. It helps me "warm up" to the practice of listening because Jesus is able to say immediately, *Yes*, or, *Of course I do*. It also helps me address any fears that might come between God and me as I come back to the essential truths of our relationship. I am his son. He loves me. We are good. Then I can move on to specific questions, and, over time, even very sober and weighty questions.

Pray in the Spirit

We are after the kind of prayer that sees results. God promised us results if we pray according to his will, meaning, in alignment with his intentions in this particular situation—not just his general goodwill, or his loving desires, but his plans in the need before us. We *will* see those prayers fulfilled. Certainly we can find a good bit of his will expressed in Scripture, and praying the Scriptures is a very powerful way to pray (we will turn there in just a moment). But the Scriptures also invite us into a conversational intimacy with God, and honestly, each new situation requiring prayer has so many little variables and puzzles to it we need to hear from God if we are to pray confidently.

Which brings us to the role of the Holy Spirit:

> In the same way, the Spirit helps us in our weakness. We do not know what we ought to pray for, but the Spirit himself intercedes for us through wordless groans. And he who searches our hearts knows the mind of the Spirit, because the Spirit intercedes for God's people in accordance with the will of God. (Rom. 8:26–27 UPDATED NIV)

> And pray in the Spirit on all occasions with all kinds of prayers and requests. (Eph. 6:18)

The Holy Spirit is always praying the will of God, so we want to be as tuned in to the Spirit as we can be. (This helps us with our emotions as well; the Spirit is tender toward our emotions but also helps us not to be ruled by them.) The Holy Spirit also empowers our prayers, making them mighty with the power of God. Paul said, "He who unites himself with the Lord is one with him in Spirit" (1 Cor. 6:17), so whenever I possibly can, I begin every prayer with personal consecration:

> Jesus—I present myself to you again, right here, right now,
> in this, for this. I consecrate to you my spirit, soul, and body,
> my heart, mind, and will. I consecrate to you my gifting,
> my seeing and perceiving. I consecrate these prayers to you.
> Wash me with your blood again; cleanse me and renew me.
> Holy Spirit—come and restore my union with Father and
> Son; come and fill these prayers.

I don't want to just jump in and start whacking away, only to find myself exhausted thirty minutes later with little to show for it. That can be so discouraging. First, I consecrate and ask the Holy Spirit to fill me. But I don't even start praying after that; second, *I ask the Spirit what to pray.* How he reveals this is as diverse and creative as the God who made the world around us. Sometimes I will simply hear a word, like, *Comfort.* So I will begin to pray for comfort. Sometimes he will bring a scripture to mind, and I will let that be the focus of my prayers. Other times he will reveal something key by a "feeling" or a sensation—I will suddenly feel overwhelmed, or discouraged, or fearful when I wasn't moments before—and in that manner he reveals to me what the person I am praying for is under.

But most of the time, he will speak to me in my heart—that "small, inner voice"—and give me direction as to what to pray. The more accustomed you become to this approach, the more the Spirit can guide your prayers in the moment, as you pray. It becomes one beautiful, intimate partnership of prayer.

Now yes—praying "in the Spirit" does sometimes imply praying with a language given to you by the Spirit, a "prayer language" as it is frequently called. Absolutely. Those are mighty prayers because they are expressions of the Holy Spirit directly to God.

> So what shall I do? I will pray with my spirit, but I will also pray with my understanding; I will sing with my spirit, but I will also sing with my understanding. (1 Cor. 14:15 UPDATED NIV)

What is interesting is that when Paul said, "Pray in the Spirit on all occasions," he went on to define what he meant by those words: "with all kinds of prayers and requests" (Eph. 6:18).

Those are *discernible* prayers, made by my mind as well as my spirit. So you see, "praying in the Spirit" does not always mean "pray in a prayer language." All those prayers Paul prayed for us in Scripture were clearly prayed with normal language because he recounts them to us in normal language. The mighty prayers of Jesus—including those Gethsemane prayers—those, too, were prayers in human language. Spirit-filled and Spirit-led prayer might involve praying with "the tongues of angels," but in many other occasions it is clearly prayer that can be understood.

So yes, absolutely—I give myself over to the Holy Spirit. I yield myself to him in every way and ask him to fill my prayers. I partner with the Spirit of God in me as I pray, for this is a partnership.

And then, I do what Elijah did—I look for the cloud on the horizon. Is this breaking through? Are we getting some break-through here? Does it feel like we're getting some results? If the person you are praying for is present in the room, ask them, "So, how are you doing now?" It feels risky, but let humility and the desire to learn guide you. Often you will get important feedback like, "When you guys started praying the resurrection over me, I could feel something starting to shift." Then you hone in on that and take it further.

Jesus—what should I pray in this? will prove revolutionizing to your prayer life. The intimacy you will experience with God will nourish your soul; it is so satisfying you will crave more and more. But your prayers will also be so much more effective. Again, God loves and honors our prayers as children, and as young men and women, but nowadays I rarely pray any other way than from, *Jesus—what do I pray?*

Thirteen

PRAYING SCRIPTURE

Who then is the one who condemns? No one. Christ Jesus who died—more than that, who was raised to life—is at the right hand of God and is also interceding for us. (Rom. 8:34 UPDATED NIV)

Because Jesus lives forever, he has a permanent priesthood. Therefore he is able to save completely those who come to God through him, because he always lives to intercede for them. (Heb. 7:24–25 UPDATED NIV)

These passages intrigue me deeply. It is a source of enormous comfort to know that Jesus is interceding for me. (Did you know that Jesus prays for you?!) But to be honest, it is also a little sobering to know that I am living in a story where Jesus *needs* to pray for me. Wouldn't you love to know what Jesus is praying over your life right now? Imagine you could agree in prayer with the Son of God—that ought to add some serious firepower to your prayers!

(I paused just now, as I wrote this, and prayed, *Jesus—I agree with everything you are praying for me right now*. And when that little "yikes" presented itself in my heart, a fear of what it might mean to agree with Jesus, I then added, *Jesus, I trust you. I trust your heart for me. I agree with you; I say yes to everything you are praying for me right now!*)

Some of what he prayed for us was recorded in the Gospels, so let's start there.

Praying with Jesus

Late in the gospel of John, as Jesus was preparing his followers for his coming departure, he prayed for them . . . and for us. When I read a passage of scripture like this one, I will agree in prayer right along with it. (I'll do so in italics, so you see what I mean.) Jesus is praying to his Father:

> I pray for them. I am not praying for the world, but for those you have given me, for they are yours. All I have is yours, and all you have is mine. And glory has come to me through them. I will remain in the world no longer, but they are still in the world, and I am coming to you. Holy Father, protect them by the power of your name—the name you gave me—so that they may be one as we are one. [*Yes, Father, yes—I pray that you would protect me by the power of your name, so that I might be one with you and with Jesus.*] . . . I am coming to you now, but I say these things while I am still in the world, so that they may have the full measure

of my joy within them. [*Father, yes—I ask for the full measure of the joy Jesus had within me; I ask you for his joy.*] I have given them your word and the world has hated them, for they are not of the world any more than I am of the world. My prayer is not that you take them out of the world but that you protect them from the evil one. They are not of the world, even as I am not of it. Sanctify them by the truth; your word is truth. [*Yes, Father, yes—protect me from the evil one; sanctify me by the truth.*] . . . My prayer is not for them alone. I pray also for those who will believe in me through their message, that all of them may be one, Father, just as you are in me and I am in you. May they also be in us so that the world may believe that you have sent me. [*Father, I receive this for my life; I agree in prayer that I might be one with Jesus, and one with you, Father.*] I have given them the glory that you gave me, that they may be one as we are one: I in them and you in me. May they be brought to complete unity to let the world know that you sent me and have loved them even as you have loved me. [*I receive the glory that you gave Jesus, which he has passed on to me, that I may be one with you, Father, just as Jesus is one with you. Jesus in me, and you in Jesus-in-me. May I be brought to complete unity with you, God, so that the world may know you sent Jesus.*] (John 17:9–23)

The passage primarily focuses on protection and union with God. (It is not, as it is often mistakenly used, a passage about church unity; the text is very clear that Jesus is talking about our union with him—a theme he was building upon two chapters earlier in John 15.) Sometimes I will take a passage like this and condense it into a prayer built on the scripture, writing it out in my journal so that I can pray it often:

Father, thank you for giving me to Jesus. I join my prayer with his—I pray that you would protect me from the evil one by the power of your name, the name of Jesus; I pray for the full measure of his joy, which is your joy; I pray you would sanctify me by the truth; I receive the glory that you gave Jesus, which he has passed on to me, that I may be one with you, Father, just as Jesus is one with you. Jesus in me, and you in Jesus-in-me. May I be brought to complete unity with you, God, so that the world may know you sent Jesus.

Now, you might think, *But that's not really my need; I need to pray for guidance, or for a job, or a prodigal daughter.* Friends, I understand, but let me assure you—whatever else your need, if you have the intimacy and the actual union of being with the Father that Jesus had, you are going to be in a wonderful place, and you will be far better positioned to sort out all those other things!

And you get to pray for that with perfect confidence and assurance, because you *know* this is the will of God for you! That is why I love praying the Scriptures. They are, of course, Spirit-breathed and thus so powerful; they also give me assurance that I am praying right in the center of God's will, which fills my prayers with confidence.

Praying for Others

When praying for someone's salvation (and talk about high-stakes prayer!), I turn to these passages for guidance and direction:

The god of this age [Satan] has blinded the minds of unbe-
lievers, so that they cannot see the light of the gospel that
displays the glory of Christ, who is the image of God. (2 Cor.
4:4 UPDATED NIV)

I keep asking that the God of our Lord Jesus Christ, the glorious Father, may give you the Spirit of wisdom and revelation,
so that you may know him better. (Eph. 1:17)

The Spirit you received does not make you slaves, so that you
live in fear again; rather, the Spirit you received brought about
your adoption to sonship. And by him we cry, *"Abba,* Father."
(Rom. 8:15 UPDATED NIV)

Let us fix our eyes on Jesus, the author and perfector of our
faith. (Heb. 12:2)

These passages are revealing crucial elements of "the way it
all works" when it comes to belief and unbelief, salvation and
deception—like the fact that Satan has blinded the person you
are praying for; that God gives us the Holy Spirit so that we
might see him, come to know him; that Jesus is the author of
faith. So I will take the truths revealed to me and turn them into
effective prayer:

Jesus—author and perfecter of our faith—I pray your
love over [name]. I pray you would become the author and
perfecter of their faith. Deliver them from the hold the
enemy has upon them; I pray that the veils he has put over
their heart would be torn away by the power of your cross,

by the power of your Spirit. Remove every veil keeping [name] from seeing you. I pray you would give them the Spirit of wisdom and revelation, that they would know you. Holy Spirit, come upon them; open the eyes of their heart, Lord, to see you as you are. I pray the spirit of sonship over them, by which they cry out Abba, Father. Forgive them their sins, Lord. Send your Spirit to them to reveal salvation to them.

And then I will circle back, and pray it again, and then again, as I warm up to the task and get in groove with the Spirit, all the time listening for the specific words Jesus would have me pray over this person in particular.

Confession

When it comes to the process of confession, Psalm 51 and this passage from John's first epistle has had enormous power in my life over the years:

> Purify me from my sins, and I will be clean;
>> wash me, and I will be whiter than snow.
> Oh, give me back my joy again;
>> you have broken me—
>> now let me rejoice.
> Don't keep looking at my sins.
>> Remove the stain of my guilt.
> Create in me a clean heart, O God.
>> Renew a loyal spirit within me. (Ps. 51:7–10 NLT)

> If we confess our sins, he is faithful and just and will forgive us
> our sins and purify us from all unrighteousness. (1 John 1:9)

Oh, how helpful it is to pray this in the midst of confession,
for when condemnation is raging (and how our enemy loves to
condemn), we rarely *feel* forgiven as we first seek forgiveness.

> Father, forgive me. You are faithful and just to forgive my
> sin and to cleanse me of all unrighteousness. Cleanse me of
> all unrighteousness here, Lord. I renounce my sin; I bring it
> under the blood of Christ for me. Purify me from my sins,
> wash me whiter than snow. Restore my joy again; remove the
> stain of my guilt. Create in me a clean heart, O God. Renew a
> loyal spirit within me.

I'll stay with it until I know my whole heart is involved; I
don't want to be going through the motions, and I deeply want
to experience restoration of my intimacy with God. And by the
way—that act of renouncing sin is vital to true confession and
repentance. As we have seen, sin opens the door for the enemy to
step in, and when we decidedly renounce the sin, we are shutting
the door. In that way, confession is first seeking forgiveness and
then slamming the door shut on further sin and on the enemy's
plans to seize opportunity through it.

One of My Favorites

This passage from Ephesians 3 is my favorite scripture to pray for
myself and for those I love:

I kneel before the Father, from whom his whole family in heaven and on earth derives its name. I pray that out of his glorious riches he may strengthen you with power through his Spirit in your inner being, so that Christ may dwell in your hearts through faith. And I pray that you, being rooted and established in love, may have power, together with all the saints, to grasp how wide and long and high and deep is the love of Christ, and to know this love that surpasses knowledge—that you may be filled to the measure of all the fullness of God. (vv. 14–19)

Did you hear that last promise?! "Filled to the measure of all the fullness of God" or, as the *New Living Translation* translates it, "filled with the fullness of life and power that comes from God." Wouldn't you love to be filled with the fullness of life and power that comes from God?! I know people who are chasing conferences and speakers all around the country trying to get a little more of that. And notice the earlier promise in the passage—strengthened with power in your inner being. Couldn't we all use a little more strength and power in our inmost beings?!

Now, as you spend a little time with the passage, praying it into your being, notice there is a progression:

I pray that from his glorious, unlimited resources he will give you mighty inner strength through his Holy Spirit.

And I pray that Christ will be more and more at home in your hearts as you trust in him.

May your roots go down deep into the soil of God's marvelous love.

And may you have the power to understand how wide, how long, how high, and how deep his love really is.

May you experience the love of Christ.

Then you will be filled with the fullness of life and power that comes from God. (Eph. 3:16–19 NLT)

And so I will pray that progression very deliberately:

Father—from whom all fatherhood derives its name—I pray that from your glorious, unlimited resources you would give me a mighty inner strength (a glorious inner strength) by the power of your Spirit in my inner being, my inmost being.

I pray that Jesus Christ will be more and more at home in my heart; I pray that my roots would go down deep into the soil of your marvelous love—that I would be rooted and grounded in love, that I would have the power to understand how wide, how long, how high, and how deep your love really is.

I pray to know, really know and experience, the love of Christ, so that I will be filled with the fullness of life and power that comes from above.

As you read through the Scriptures and something grabs you for yourself or another person, pray it! It will be fun to search through the Bible finding the prayers prayed over you, finding all the wonderful promises given to us as believers, and then praying them!

Caveat

Now, yes—we do need to be careful we do not seize upon random scriptures as God's personal promises to us. I know a number of people who have tried, and it has wounded their faith when God did not deliver as they seemed to think he had promised. One classic example is the passage, "Train up a child in the way he should go, even when he is old he will not depart from it" (Prov. 22:6 NASB). This is a *principle*, not a promise, as reality has proven thousands of times over. Children from wonderful homes go prodigal; children from awful homes turn out to be missionaries. By all means pray this passage, but with the humility of knowing you are not claiming a binding promise but rather leaning into a principle of Scripture. (By the way, when praying for children, the earlier prayer from Ephesians 3 would be far more effective.)

The Scriptures are not a random grab bag of passages we select willy-nilly like a child trick-or-treating; we do need to be careful about that. Simply because God promised David that his heirs would always sit on the throne doesn't mean I can just grab that for my life. The context of a passage will give you clarity on who it is meant for, whether it is a promise or a principle, whether that promise is for every person or for believers or for a moment in history when God was doing something specific with a particular person. (Once again, in our handling of the Word of God, we are growing in maturity.)

Having offered this word of caution, I do believe the Scriptures are "living and active," that God can and does apply passages and promises to us as individuals even though their origins may have been in a different historical moment. Many of the prophesies and promises of the Old Testament find their fulfillment in the New Testament—certainly for Christ, but also for his church.

When God said to Israel, "you will be called by a new name that the mouth of the LORD will bestow" (Isa. 62:2), it was true over them at the time and it is true over us now, for he has called us saints and not sinners, friends and not servants, sons and daughters. Simon becomes Peter, Saul becomes Paul, and Ed down the street gets a new name from God as well.

And while not every word spoken in the Bible is a direct promise to us—it was Abraham who would become the father of many nations, not Ed down the street—still, we see in these passages the kind of God he is and the kinds of things he does; they give us insight into how he interacts with the world.

> I will go before you
> and will level the mountains;
> I will break down gates of bronze
> and cut through bars of iron.
> I will give you hidden treasures,
> riches stored in secret places,
> so that you may know that I am the LORD,
> the God of Israel, who summons you by name. (Isa.
> 45:2–3 UPDATED NIV)

The passage was originally spoken to Cyrus, who was king of Persia at the time. Nevertheless it is a powerful expression of God's ability to "go before" us as well. I don't see it so much as a specific promise but as a reflection on the kind of thing God does; this is how he acts. I know from the gospel of John that Jesus promised he would go before me: "The one who enters by the gate is the shepherd of the sheep. The gatekeeper opens the gate for him, and the sheep listen to his voice. He calls his own sheep by name and leads them out. When he has brought out all his own, he goes on ahead of them, and his sheep follow him because they know his voice" (10:2–4 UPDATED NIV).

So yes, by all means, when I am facing an obstacle I will pray,

> Jesus, go before me and level mountains; break through gates of bronze and cut through bars of iron here. Give to me the treasures hidden in secret places. Go before me and break through every barrier, Lord!

My attitude is, "This is my God; this is how he acts; you can do this, Jesus! I'm praying you would do it for me!" The Scriptures are mighty and Spirit-breathed, and they will lend both precision and power to your prayer life. As you read the Bible, by all means take it in and let it minister to your soul. But also pray it! This is how we get active and begin to wield "the sword of the Spirit," which has devastating consequences against our enemy.

Fourteen

WARFARE PRAYER

A boy with a BB gun on his grandfather's ranch, and the entire summer before him, is the richest man in the world.

I was eight years old. My grandfather had bought me a pump-model rifle and one of those milk cartons full of BBs, and I had endless acres of irrigation ditches to explore, hunting frogs. They are naturally camouflaged little buggers—all green and brown blotches just the color of muddy water and moss—and they're smart enough to lie very still until you are almost upon them. For they know if they move, they will reveal their location (a lesson learned by many a lost frog, thanks to the herons that have hunted them since time gone by).

My early successes were minimal. I tried sneaking up, but the little amphibians would remain hidden in the reeds and mossy bays, laying stock-still, and my untrained eyes couldn't pick them out. The technique involved walking slowly along the banks, intentionally disturbing the frogs but not scaring the bejesus out of them, so that they would dive or hop or swish and catch my eye, and then I could stand still as the heron and wait for them to resurface and take my shot.

It was the beginning of a boy's education in one of the fundamental lessons of life: there is a way things work.

Those were idyllic summers for me, and every memory I have of them is "Apparell'd in celestial light," as Wordsworth beautifully described it.[1] Every memory except two. My grandfather contracted brain cancer when I was seventeen, and he died very quickly. That was a summer I do not cherish. But earlier, when I was around twelve, still a boy, I had a summer of nightmares. Pop and Gram slept in the one upstairs bedroom and I slept in the basement. It was lovely and cool downstairs. But that summer I had a number of scary and inexplicable encounters which at the time I had no worldview to explain. Now I know it was demonic attack. Needless to say, they were frightening.

A few months ago—more than forty years later—I came to an older saint for prayer because a friend had recommended him as remarkably gifted in prayer for the healing of the soul, and I knew my soul needed some tending to. We did not talk about my life story; he asked very few questions that a counselor normally would ask. He chose instead to turn to Jesus and invite his presence to bring his healing ministry. "Where is this distress coming from, Lord?" Immediately I was taken back to a memory I had long forgotten—that summer in the basement at the ranch.

Honestly, I had completely forgotten the entire thing. But Jesus lovingly took me back there to reveal where fear had gotten in.

"What is the lie that took root there, Lord?" the old sage asked. My heart answered: *I am alone and exposed; I am not protected.* "And what are you saying to John to do with that?" Jesus responded, *Break agreement with the lie; renounce it.* So I did. Such a simple act, but it felt monumental because when I was twelve, I made deep agreements with the fear, and for forty years it had gone unattended to. *Banish the fear, in my name.* We commanded the spirit of fear to leave and never return. *Now invite my healing love there.* We did, and it was as if I could feel Jesus enter that basement room, in my memory of that time and place, and his presence in my soul, where those memories remained very much alive, made everything all right. Jesus entered into the memory and made it his own; he comforted that twelve-year-old part of me, which I had long forgotten.

A door was closed to fear that day, and I have enjoyed the relief of it since.

The Victory Has Been Won

Now we turn to the form of prayer that often brings the most dramatic and immediate results—prayer that banishes the enemy. It is actually a simple form of prayer, and very effective. The reason more people don't enjoy its wonderful fruits is either because they don't believe we are at war (a worldview that takes massive amounts of denial to sustain) or because they feel intimidated by the subject. So let me make this clear—the enemy *always* tries to keep you from praying against him, as Jesus taught us to pray, because he knows once you learn how to do this, his gig is up. Really—this is extremely simple and yet quite effective, just as we read in Acts:

> Once when we were going to the place of prayer, we were
> met by a slave girl who had a spirit by which she predicted

the future. She earned a great deal of money for her owners by fortune-telling. This girl followed Paul and the rest of us, shouting, "These men are servants of the Most High God, who are telling you the way to be saved." She kept this up for many days. Finally Paul became so troubled that he turned around and said to the spirit, "In the name of Jesus Christ I command you to come out of her!" At that moment the spirit left her. (Acts 16:16–18)

And that was that. No one needed to shout; no one foamed at the mouth; no one's head spun on a swivel. No special effects you see in horror films are recorded here. Paul simply used the authority we all share with Jesus, and the enemy had to leave. It really is that basic.

Which brings us back to what we were exploring in chapter 5—the overthrow of the kingdom of darkness, and the authority given to Jesus Christ. How Jesus is actively reigning now *until* he has completely vanquished the enemy—beach by beach, tunnel by tunnel. And he has clearly called us up into this fight. When Satan was cast down from the heavens, he declared war on the church; that includes you. "Then the dragon was enraged at the woman and went off to make war against . . . those who obey God's commandments and hold to the testimony of Jesus" (Rev. 12:17). We are at war, whether you choose to believe it or not. I said I believe that part of the reason God has left it to be done this way is because he is growing us up; we too must learn to rule and reign.

The wonderful news is that the cross of Jesus Christ disarmed all foul spirits—the "powers and authorities" (Col. 2:15), meaning the evil one himself, and all those fallen angels in his armies, like the prince of the Persian kingdom. Having cast them down, all authority was given to Jesus. And then—I suggested that at this point trumpets ought to ring out and banners unfurl—he gave his majestic authority to us: "I have given you authority . . . to overcome all the power of the enemy" (Luke 10:19).

Notice he doesn't take away the attack; rather, he gives us the authority we need to overcome it. Far better to learn how to shut it down than let it wreak havoc in your kingdom unchecked and unchallenged. You have everything you need to live a life free from Satan's assaults. The demons know your authority in Jesus; they know that if you banish them, they have to obey. Every time they are commanded to in Scripture, they obey. So of course they try to make you feel as though you don't really want to pray like this. They nearly always send distraction or confusion, all sorts of feelings like, *Really—do we really have to deal with this?* Yes, my friends, you do. In fact, you are commanded to fight:

> Submit yourselves, then, to God. Resist the devil, and he will flee from you. (James 4:7)

> Be self-controlled and alert. Your enemy the devil prowls around like a roaring lion looking for someone to devour. Resist him, standing firm in the faith, because you know that your brothers throughout the world are undergoing the same kind of sufferings. (1 Peter 5:8–9)

Resist. Fight back. Take your stand. Scripture is very clear on this point. First, Jesus models it; then the disciples do it, and then Paul and the early church. To make it all perfectly clear, the command to fight is also written down in black and white. This is part of what it means to be a Christian. I am amazed by the hemming and hawing and dodging Christians will go through to avoid this: "It's not your job to resist the devil—that's Jesus' job." No—you have been commanded to resist. "The devil is a toothless lion." No—scripture says he can steal, kill, and destroy; it says he can devour. "Warfare isn't necessary when we focus on worship; the devil never rushes into the throne room of God." Worship *is* a powerful tool against the enemy. But, friends, you do not live in the throne room of God; you live your days here on this earth, in the midst of war, and "your brothers throughout the world are undergoing" spiritual attack (1 Peter 5:9). Including you. The war is all around us, friends, and getting worse.

But my goodness—do we really need to be commanded to learn warfare prayer?! That's like saying, "I won't do anything about this infection in my body; I'd rather be sick." Or, "I won't try the gates of my prison to see if I might go free; I'd rather sit in darkness." The utter relief of getting free from the attacks of the enemy are worth whatever effort this requires. And, friends, in most situations, this doesn't require a lot of effort:

Then he went down to Capernaum, a town in Galilee, and on the Sabbath began to teach the people. They were amazed at his teaching, because his message had authority.

In the synagogue there was a man possessed by a demon, an evil spirit. He cried out at the top of his voice, "Ha! What do you want with us, Jesus of Nazareth? Have you come to destroy us? I know who you are—the Holy One of God!"

"Be quiet!" Jesus said sternly. "Come out of him!" Then the demon threw the man down before them all and came out without injuring him.

All the people were amazed and said to each other, "What is this teaching? With authority and power he gives orders to evil spirits and they come out!" And the news about him spread throughout the surrounding area. (Luke 4:31–37)

Jesus rebukes it, banishes it, and that's that. Any questions? This is the model Jesus has provided for us; it is the same model Paul based his prayers on, with wonderful results. I'm curious—why do we accept Jesus as a model for forgiving others, or loving God as Father, or caring for the poor, but not in the simple matter of dealing with the enemy? His disciples seized upon this with *joy*:

The seventy-two returned with joy and said, "Lord, even the demons submit to us in your name."
He replied, "I saw Satan fall like lightning from heaven. I have given you authority to trample on snakes and scorpions and to overcome all the power of the enemy." (Luke 10:17–19)

This is going to provide a lot of relief for a lot of people. Let me explain how it works because as you understand this type of prayer, it doesn't magnify Satan's role in your life; it deepens your understanding of the victory Jesus has already won for us! The work of Christ gives us everything we need to triumph over foul spirits and demonic attacks:

For he has rescued us from the dominion of darkness and brought us into the kingdom of the Son he loves, in whom we have redemption, the forgiveness of sins. (Col. 1:13–14)

When you were dead in your sins and in the uncircumcision

of your sinful nature, God made you alive with Christ. He forgave us all our sins, having canceled the written code, with its regulations, that was against us and that stood opposed to us; he took it away, nailing it to the cross. And having disarmed the powers and authorities, he made a public spectacle of them, triumphing over them by the cross. (Col. 2:13–15)

Since the children have flesh and blood, he too shared in their humanity so that by his death he might destroy him who holds the power of death—that is, the devil—and free those who all their lives were held in slavery by their fear of death. (Heb. 2:14–15)

Now have come the salvation and the power and the kingdom of our God, and the authority of his Christ. For the accuser of our brothers . . . has been hurled down. They overcame him by the blood of the Lamb and by the word of their testimony; they did not love their lives so much as to shrink from death. (Rev. 12:10–11)

We have absolutely nothing to fear. Jesus has secured our everlasting victory over the enemy, whatever his attack might be. We have everything we need.

Enforcing That Victory

A young woman we love called to ask for prayer. She was being tormented at night with fear and anxiety; it was robbing her of sleep and taking a terrible toll. We love offering this kind of prayer because the results are oftentimes immediate, which strengthens the faith of the believer to press into Christ in prayer for themselves.

We paused to listen, asking Jesus what we were dealing with, and—most importantly—how did the fear get in? There is almost always some reason the demons think they have a right to be there; it might be sin, but it might be something else. In this case, Jesus made us aware of two things. First off, fear had been a major issue in her mother's life; it was a family battle, something our friend Cammie had sort of "inherited." Second, Jesus gently reminded us that Cammie is a perfectionist; her fear of failure provided an open door for the enemy to get in. That gave us further direction in prayer.

Here is how we prayed:

> We declare and we proclaim that Cammie belongs to Jesus Christ. She has been bought with the blood of Christ. Her life belongs to Jesus Christ and to no other. Satan—you have no hold and no claim upon this woman's life.

As you proclaim the truth, the demons begin to cower. We then led Cammie in renouncing the ways she had given fear a claim (we first submit to God, as James says, then resist). She also renounced her family's "agreement" with fear:

> Jesus, I renounce my perfectionism. I renounce trying to secure myself through a perfect performance. You are my only Savior, my security; you are my safe place. Forgive me for giving the enemy a foothold in my life. I renounce every agreement I have made with fear. I place my trust in you,

God. I also renounce my family's agreement with fear; I renounce the claim they have given fear in our household.

Having renounced the enemy's claims to be there, we were able to bind and banish the spirit of fear, wielding the sword of the Spirit:

We declare and we proclaim that God has not given Cammie a spirit of fear. "For you did not receive a spirit that makes you a slave again to fear, but you received the Spirit of sonship. And by him we cry, 'Abba, Father'" (Rom. 8:15). "For God has not given us a spirit of fear, but of power and of love and of a sound mind" (2 Tim. 1:7 NKJV). We therefore bring the cross and blood of the Lord Jesus Christ against all fear and anxiety; we cut you off in the name of the Lord. By the authority of Jesus Christ we command all fear and anxiety bound and banished—banished to the judgment Jesus Christ has for you. Leave Cammie, and never return. In the mighty name of Jesus Christ our Lord.

And that was that. Really. Sure—fear tried to get back in a few more times over the next week or two, but Cammie kept her stand in Jesus Christ, and fear had to go. This is the basic procedure for warfare prayer:

Step One: Identify the spirit.

Demons are fallen angels, foul spirits; they are rebellious by nature and they do everything they can to try and maintain their oppression. You have to be specific with them. It is fascinating to me that in his encounter with the man in the tombs, Jesus had to get specific with the enemy to make him leave:

When Jesus stepped ashore, he was met by a demon-possessed man from the town. For a long time this man had not worn clothes or lived in a house, but had lived in the tombs. When he saw Jesus, he cried out and fell at his feet, shouting at the top of his voice, "What do you want with me, Jesus, Son of the Most High God? I beg you, don't torture me!" For Jesus had commanded the evil spirit to come out of the man. Many times it had seized him, and though he was chained hand and foot and kept under guard, he had broken his chains and had been driven by the demon into solitary places.

Jesus asked him, "What is your name?"

"Legion," he replied, because many demons had gone into him. (Luke 8:27–30)

Interesting—in verse 29, the spirit is freaking out but it has not left, even though the passage says Jesus "had" commanded (past tense) the spirit to leave. The story is told with exactly the same language in the gospel of Mark as well. Apparently, his first command was not fully effective, so Jesus then demands to know its name. When they identify themselves as "legion" (meaning, many spirits), Christ is then able to send all of them away. Like the story of the blind man who only saw "men like trees" when Jesus first gives him the healing touch, this story is also for our benefit.

We have found it helpful and often necessary to name the foul spirits as we banish them. Fuzzy and unspecific prayers see fuzzy and unspecific results. God is growing us up. There is a way things work.

Identifying the spirit is usually obvious, as with fear, or shame, or feeling overwhelmed. You just look at what it is doing—is the person fearful, or wracked with shame, or utterly overwhelmed? There you go. But we often ask Jesus what is going on and let him guide us as well.

Step Two: Renounce the enemy's claim.

There is some reason, however illegitimate, why the enemy is present. As we have seen, sin certainly opens the door to demonic attack. If you are trying to get free from an attack of lust, you must first renounce all the ways you have lusted (including the use of pornography or fantasy). Bringing those sins under the blood of Christ breaks the enemy's power to use them as a right to oppress.

But many other things give the enemy a claim, including unresolved emotional issues: "'In your anger do not sin': Do not let the sun go down while you are still angry, and do not give the devil a foothold" (Eph. 4:26–27).

The letter is written to Christians; it says Christians can give the devil a foothold (thus correcting the mistaken theology that Christians can't be oppressed). If you hold on to trauma, rage, or guilt for years, it is likely the enemy is going to use those unaddressed issues as an opportunity to oppress you. My story of fear when I was twelve, left unaddressed, gave the enemy an opportunity until I took that opportunity away through intentional prayer.

Often, in order to renounce the enemy's claim, we, or the person we are praying for, need to "break agreements" with the attack. In other words, we renounce the agreements we have been giving to fear, or guilt, or what have you.

Once again it is helpful to ask Jesus what the enemy's claim is; let Christ reveal how the enemy got a foothold. Pausing to listen has revealed many surprising and helpful things to us (I had completely forgotten those summer nightmares at my grandfather's ranch until Jesus brought it back). Then we can renounce it.

Step Three: Bring the work of Christ against it.

So much of our discussion on the Prayer of Intervention has been built on the understanding of delegation. The most startling example of delegation is God's decision to leave the spread of the gospel to us(!). Salvation was won by Christ, but we have a role in bringing it to the world. In the same way Jesus won the victory over Satan, but we have a role in *enforcing* that victory in specific situations.

Proclaiming, invoking, and enforcing prove most effective here. We proclaim the truth—that is the sword of the Spirit, the Word of God. We invoke the authority of Christ over the specific need—that is how we bring the rule of Jesus back over the place now being claimed by Satan. We enforce the work and authority of Christ directly and specifically against the oppressors—that is how we get the enemy to leave. Demons (often referred to as "foul spirits") are belligerent, deceitful, and rebellious. They need to be confronted with the triumph of Jesus Christ.

Step Four: Send the foul spirits to the judgment Jesus has for them.

There are a variety of ways foul spirits are rebuked in the New Testament: some are sent to the abyss (Luke 8:31; Rev. 20:2–3); some are sent to "dungeons to be held for judgment" (2 Peter 2:4); some are simply "banished" as we saw Paul do in Acts 16. Rather than trying to sort all that out, unless Jesus gives you specific orders, we find it simple enough to send the spirits "to the judgment Jesus has for you." And off they go.

Now—because we are in a vicious war, and late in that war, you will encounter situations where the spirit refuses to leave. (They are rebellious spirits after all—that's how they became demons.) In those cases, we call down the discipline of Christ upon them, or the judgment of Christ upon them, right then and there. The Psalms are filled with this sort of commanding:

> I pursued my enemies and overtook them;
>> I did not turn back till they were destroyed.
> I crushed them so that they could not rise;
>> they fell beneath my feet.
> You armed me with strength for battle;
>> you made my adversaries bow at my feet.
> You made my enemies turn their backs in flight,
>> and I destroyed my foes. (Ps. 18:37–40)

We also saw Paul do this back in Acts 13:11 when he rebuked Elymas the sorcerer: "Now the hand of the Lord is against you." This has proven necessary in some situations. We love to proclaim to stubborn spirits, "Even the demons submit to us in your name!" (Luke 10:17) and, "Every knee will bow . . . and every tongue will confess that Jesus Christ is Lord" (Phil. 2:10–11 NLT), and we keep doing it until they submit and obey.

The Warfare of Others

Spiritual warfare often tries to work like a computer virus—it loves to transfer around to as many people as it can, infecting whole households or even churches. You can witness this with great clarity when you are standing outside of it. You will step into certain fellowships and immediately feel an arrogant attitude, or perhaps something that feels very "religious" and stifling; perhaps there is a sense of guilt overwhelming the group. You've seen the same thing in family systems—how a particular sin or brokenness will play out down through a family line, such as divorce, infidelity, pornography and sexual sin, alcoholism, violence, poverty, shame, fear. Somebody's sin opened the door, and because the spiritual realm works on authority, the enemy will seize the opportunity of the sin (often repeated and habitual sins) and will try to oppress all those within the "system."

Oftentimes you'll walk away from a meeting, a gathering, an intervention, a party, or a family reunion and feel as though you are leaving with something that you did not come there with. Though you felt fine when you entered, you now feel guilty, or you feel the religious suffocation, or the arrogance, or bitterness. I was just counseling a couple who was struggling with a great deal of anger, and afterward I found myself tempted to get angry on the road, angry at my dog, angry at anything that moved. Once again the cross is our rescue: "May I never boast except in the cross of our Lord Jesus Christ, through which the world has been crucified to me, and I to the world" (Gal. 6:14).

The Greek word here for "the world" we are crucified to is *kosmos*. It is quite an encompassing term, including all the inhabitants of the earth, mankind, the human race. It also refers to the ungodly, the mass of mankind alienated from God. You are crucified to that controlling mother, or angry boss; you are crucified to that church holding to arrogant sin or false humility.

You will therefore find it very helpful to bring the cross of Christ between you and others, especially when you feel their warfare is trying to jump on you or in cases of unhealthy emotional and spiritual ties:

> I bring the cross of my Lord Jesus Christ between me and
> ____. I have been crucified to ___ and they have been
> crucified to me. By the cross I break all unhealthy ties and
> every unholy bond with ___. I command their sin, warfare,
> and corruption back to the throne of Christ over their life,
> and I forbid it to transfer to me, in Jesus' name. I allow only
> the love of God, the Spirit of God, and the kingdom of God
> between us. In Jesus' mighty name, and by his authority.

The beauty is, the cross never prevents love from passing between us, never prevents the Spirit of God from coming between us. The cross only cuts off unhealthy things, so there is never any fear in bringing it between you and the *kosmos*.

Curses and Judgments

The Moabites said to the elders of Midian, "This horde is going to lick up everything around us, as an ox licks up the grass of the field."

So Balak son of Zippor, who was king of Moab at that time, sent messengers to summon Balaam son of Beor, who was at Pethor, near the River, in his native land. Balak said:

"A people has come out of Egypt; they cover the face of the land and have settled next to me. Now come and put a curse on these people, because they are too powerful for me. Perhaps then I will be able to defeat them and drive them out of the country. For I know that those you bless are blessed, and those you curse are cursed." (Num. 22:4–6)

Years ago I kept having repeated bouts of heart and chest pains (not something you want to ignore). On several occasions they became so severe I went to the emergency room, was immediately hospitalized, and was taken through a battery of tests. Despite exhaustive attempts by good doctors to identify the cause of the chest pains, on all three occasions they found nothing. "I'm sorry, Mr. Eldredge, but your heart is as strong as an ox. There is nothing physically wrong with you." I left with a clean bill of health, but my heart was still experiencing sharp pains.

Then I went to see a man who was well educated in spiritual warfare—a "father" who had gained wisdom on the way things work in this arena. We had never met before, and he knew nothing of my story; but as soon as we sat down together, he said, "Are you aware that there is a curse on your heart?" I had never heard of such a thing. I said no, to which he replied, "Well—have you been experiencing heart pains and such?" "I thought I was dying of a heart attack—does that count?" He explained that witches had placed curses on my physical heart; then he prayed for me, to break those curses, and the symptoms went away. Over the past fifteen years those symptoms have reappeared on a few occasions, but knowing how to pray, I was able to break them off myself. What joyful relief!

The Scriptures take blessing and cursing *very* seriously; they are considered real and actual forces, with real and lasting effects:

Melchizedek blessed Abram with this blessing: "Blessed be Abram by God Most High, Creator of heaven and earth. And blessed be God Most High, who has defeated your enemies for you." (Gen. 14:19–20 NLT)

"But look," Jacob replied to Rebekah, "my brother, Esau, is a hairy man, and my skin is smooth. What if my father touches me? He'll see that I'm trying to trick him, and then he'll curse me instead of blessing me." (Gen. 27:11–12 NLT)

Bless those who persecute you; bless and do not curse. (Rom. 12:14)

If anyone does not love the Lord—a curse be on him. (1 Cor. 16:22)

All who rely on observing the law are under a curse, for it is written: "Cursed is everyone who does not continue to do everything written in the Book of the Law." (Gal. 3:10)

With the tongue we praise our Lord and Father, and with it we curse men, who have been made in God's likeness. (James 3:9)

Remember—there is a way things work in the spiritual realm, just as there is a way things work in the physical. Blessing and cursing works; it has powerful effects for good or for evil. Jesus says bless those who curse you; he did not say, "Don't worry about curses; they aren't real." In fact, he cursed a fig tree, and the next day it withered.

We live in a world at war. Men and women curse each other, sometimes unintentionally, and sometimes very intentionally. Jesus has his allies in the human race; they are called Christians. Satan also has allies he has won over in the human race; some of them take great pleasure in cursing Christians. The curse on my heart had apparently been brought on by one of Satan's allies. This sort of warfare is common throughout the world; only in the "enlightened" Western world has the power of this been forgotten or dismissed.

Tragically, Christians do a good bit of cursing one another. Someone just posted on our ministry Facebook page a message along the lines of, "You are heretics, doomed to judgment!" They are clearly judging us; they may in fact be outright cursing us, *wishing judgment upon us.* When someone says to you, "I pray that you fail," or, "I pray that God brings suffering upon you so that you learn to obey," they are in fact speaking words of harm over you; they are cursing you. Remember—"Death and life are in the power of the tongue" (Prov. 18:21 KJV).

Christians will even go so far as to curse one another in prayer, praying things like, "Humble them, Lord! Break them! I call down your judgment upon them." Or, "I pray their ministry stumbles, Lord; I pray they would be thwarted at every step." This is extremely sinful and damaging.

Cursing is done with purposeful intent; they are words spoken with malice, words spoken to bring harm. "Judgments" are far more common, but they are destructive too. "You are so arrogant," is a word of judgment; so are words like, "I hate you!" and, "You won't amount to anything; you will make the family business fail." Judgments are like low-grade curses. We must take these things seriously because they bring harm upon our lives, our health, our churches and ministries. The Scripture takes them very seriously.

And once again, it is the victory of Christ that breaks the powers of sin and darkness: "Christ redeemed us from the curse of the law by becoming a curse for us, for it is written: 'Cursed is everyone who is hung on a tree'" (Gal. 3:13).

Jesus was cursed in your place; Jesus was judged in your place. His blood and sacrifice cancel all other claims of judgment or cursing against you. So here is how we pray against curses and judgments (a fuller version of this prayer is available at ransomedheart.com):

I proclaim that "Christ redeemed us from the curse of the law by becoming a curse for us, for it is written: 'Cursed is everyone who is hung on a tree'" (Gal. 3:13). In the name of the Lord Jesus Christ, I now bring the fullness of his cross, death, blood, and sacrifice against every curse and judgment. I bring Jesus Christ cursed for me against all curses and judgments that have been raised against me—written, spoken, unspoken, or transferred to me. [If you know what the exact curses are, it helps to name them. For example, "all curses of death," or, "all curses on my marriage or my health," etc.] In the name and by the blood of Jesus Christ, I break the power and hold of every curse and judgment that has come to me through words spoken against me. Through the blood of Jesus Christ, I am free. Thank you, Jesus, for setting me free. I order these curses and claims utterly disarmed and dismantled now, through the power of the blood of Jesus Christ, and in his name.

The Glorious Freedom

Warfare prayer is not a "back-up" category when all else fails. It is not a specialty form of prayer for the uniquely called or gifted.

Yes—there are some who become "experts" in this field, just as there are some who become especially trained to heal or to preach the gospel. But we are all called to preach the gospel; we are all called to resist the enemy. You are living out your daily life in the context of war. The men and women who choose to equip themselves and become practiced in warfare prayer are the ones who enjoy the greatest freedom and breakthrough—the "glorious freedom of the children of God" (Rom. 8:21).

In fact, by choosing to rule in this category of reality (there is a way things work), you will discover a wonderful surprise—all those passages in Scripture that shout with praises of triumph and victory, all those hallelujahs with fireworks going off will suddenly make sense to you:

> I will give thanks to you, LORD, with all my heart;
>> I will tell of all your wonderful deeds.
> I will be glad and rejoice in you;
>> I will sing the praises of your name, O Most High.
> My enemies turn back;
>> they stumble and perish before you. (Ps. 9:1–3 NLT)

These fabulous passages—and there are *thousands* in both the Old and New Testaments—have been a puzzle and irritation to most postmodern Christians. Until they discover the reality of the war, and the power of wielding the triumph of Christ and his authority. Then they begin singing and praising like this! The experience is like discovering the missing chapters to your story.

Now, I do not mean to minimize difficult situations of spiritual attack. We have faced some very serious attack over the years, and we know many who have as well. So by saying this is typically a simple and effective form of prayer, I do not mean to imply it is *always* simple. But it is always effective, especially as we operate as sons and daughters, seated with Christ in authority at the Father's right hand. I have listed some resources for further study below. Freedom is your *right*. For as Paul urged in Galatians, "It is for freedom that Christ has set us free. . . . Do not let yourselves be burdened again by a yoke of slavery" (Gal. 5:1). Do not "let"—the choice is up to you.

For further study:

Neil Anderson: *Victory over the Darkness* and *The Bondage Breaker*

Dr. Ed Murphy: *The Handbook for Spiritual Warfare*

Timothy Warner: *Spiritual Warfare: Victory over the Powers of This Dark World*

Ransomed Heart Ministries: "A Battle to Fight" and "Finding Freedom" (audio)

Fifteen

INNER HEALING—
RESTORING THE SOUL

Now we have come in our prayer tutorial to what I believe is
the most beautiful form of prayer—prayer for the healing
of the heart and soul. At its very best, all prayer is deep communion, drawing us into intimacy and union with our God. When that
intimacy and union reaches the damaged places within us, it is like
the spring showers that come to Death Valley—wildflowers burst
forth from barren ground, and the land looks like Eden again. The
inner healing that occurs is more beautiful than anything in nature
that has taken your breath away. For the heart and soul of a human
being is worth far more than all the beautiful places in the world.

(I doubt you believe that about your wounded heart, but
consider—Jesus did not die for pine trees. He fully intends to restore
this earth he made, but *you* are the prize he ransomed with his life.)

Prayer for inner healing is worth volumes in itself, but I cannot
ignore it here; the need is too great, the fruits far too wonderful

to pass it by unaddressed. I believe I can put into your hands the essential tools—for here, too, there is a way things work—and with a little experimentation you will soon discover how accessible this form of prayer actually is. Jesus *loves* to partner with us in this most sacred place; he is most eager to come and make himself known here.

Healing the Ravages of This War

In the past six months, as our team has brought healing prayer to men and women, we have heard enough stories of pain and heartache to sink a battleship: a boy sexually abused by his father nightly for five years, a woman whose husband attempted to murder her, repeated abandonment, multiple suicide efforts, paranoia, chronic pain that nothing could ease, trauma, rejection. Friends, we live in a brutal world. This is a love story, but it is set in the midst of a terrible and violent war. Very few of us pass through this life without damage inflicted upon our hearts and souls.

You are more than a body, by the way—you have a heart, and a soul. Our scientific age has caused many Christians to adopt a very medical model for treating humanity. When a headache hits, they automatically reach for ibuprofen, not prayer. The thought that a headache might be a spiritual attack is not even a consideration. So, too, we look to medicate emotional problems when what is actually happening may not be medical at all (or, may express itself physically but have a "soulful" root).*

---

* I believe in medication, by the way. Some of the emotional distress people experience is due to the imbalance of delicate chemical symmetry in the body and brain; treating those imbalances has brought relief to millions.

We won't be going into deep technicalities of what comprises heart and what comprises soul; those distinctions are not necessary for most cases of healing. You don't have to understand how and why sleep works in order to enjoy it and be restored by it. Your body was nourished by that banana you enjoyed without you understanding how the potassium was assimilated into your cells. The deep mysteries are worth exploring if you cannot find resolution for sleep distresses, just as the mysteries of the heart and soul are worth studying if you have encountered something that cannot receive healing without further understanding, or if you have a ministry in healing prayer. I will include a few recommendations at the chapter's end.

But let me offer this clarity: First, you have a body, a soul, and a spirit. "May God himself, the God of peace, sanctify you through and through. May your whole spirit, soul and body be kept blameless at the coming of our Lord Jesus Christ" (1 Thess. 5:23).

Spirit, soul, and body; *pneuma*, *psuche*, *soma* in the Greek. Three clearly distinct realms of the human being.

Your spirit is the life breath of God within you, giving life to both body and soul. It is the life force of God within you, animating both body and soul. Your soul is comprised of a number of capacities, including heart, mind, and will. Your spirit is the sunshine; your soul the stained-glass window it shines through.

Your soul is actually a region of vast mystery and beauty, filled with memories and capacities far beyond the reckoning of the average person educated in the scientific era. Both the Old and New Testaments address the heart and soul as distinct entities (I believe the heart is the seat of your soul, or the center of your soul). They are very real "things" and can be wounded deeply, as anyone who has been heartbroken can tell you. As your own soul will tell you, if you will but listen. When the old prophet Simeon took the baby Jesus into his arms at the temple in Jerusalem (this was before the flight to Egypt), he said something ominous to Jesus' mother: "This child is destined to cause the falling and rising of many in Israel, and to be a sign that will be spoken against, so that the thoughts of many hearts will be revealed. And a sword will pierce your own soul too" (Luke 2:34–35).

Watching her beloved son tortured and executed was going to be so devastating, the damage to Mary's soul would be as real as if a sword had run through it. This is validating for the scripture to acknowledge this, for many of you know exactly what I am trying now to reveal—that actual damage is done to the inner places of your being. A good part of the Cry of the Heart is in fact a cry for God to heal this very sort of damage:

> Come near and rescue me;
>> redeem me because of my foes.
> You know how I am scorned, disgraced and shamed;
>> all my enemies are before you.
> Scorn has broken my heart
>> and has left me helpless;
> I looked for sympathy, but there was none,
>> for comforters, but I found none. (Ps. 69:18–20)

Scorn in this case has broken the mighty warrior David's heart; rejection will do that, as many people know. Betrayal is another heartbreaker.

> Reckless words pierce like a sword,
>> but the tongue of the wise brings healing. (Prov. 12:18)

I will be glad and rejoice in your love,
>   for you saw my affliction
>   and knew the anguish of my soul.
> You have not handed me over to the enemy
>   but have set my feet in a spacious place.
> Be merciful to me, O LORD, for I am in distress;
>   my eyes grow weak with sorrow,
>   my soul and my body with grief. (Ps. 31:7–9)

My soul is in deep anguish. (6:3 UPDATED NIV)

Relieve the troubles of my heart
>   and free me from my anguish. (25:17 UPDATED NIV)

My heart is blighted and withered like grass. (102:4)
My heart is wounded within me. (109:22)

You get the idea; the heart and soul can be wounded, damaged in the same way that the physical body can be. As if I needed to tell you any of this. The glorious news is that God restores the soul; he heals the broken heart:

The LORD is my shepherd . . .
>   he restores my soul. (Ps. 23:1, 3)

He heals the brokenhearted
>   and binds up their wounds. (Ps. 147:3)
He has sent me to bind up the brokenhearted. (Isa. 61:1)

When you experience this for yourself, or minister it through prayer to another human being, there is nothing like it on earth.

For the search for wholeness compels every person, every hour of their lives, whether they know it or not. We ache to be made whole again. And only one Person who ever walked this earth can do this for the heart and soul he created himself.

The Essence of Healing

As we explore the many beautiful and intimate ways Jesus comes to heal our inner beings, keep in mind that whatever the damage may be, in any realm of your inner being, the essence of healing prayer is always to facilitate the presence of Jesus into the specific places of damage. Whatever else might be involved, it always begins with, "Jesus, come into this and heal."

Oswald Chambers, a man who wrote profoundly and elegantly on prayer, made a radical statement when he said, "The idea of prayer is not in order to get answers from God." Good heavens—it's not? What then is the purpose? "Prayer is perfect and complete oneness with God."[1] A mighty truth is being uncovered here.

Oneness with God is the goal of our existence. It's not merely to believe in God, although that is better than not believing in him. It is not merely to trust in God, though that is far better than simply believing in God. It is not even to worship God, which is higher still. In some of his last words to us—his *prayers* for us—Jesus raised this to the highest place:

> My prayer is not for them alone. I pray also for those who will believe in me through their message, that all of them may be

one, Father, just as you are in me and I am in you. May they also be in us so that the world may believe that you have sent me. I have given them the glory that you gave me, that they may be one as we are one—I in them and you in me—so that they may be brought to complete unity. Then the world will know that you sent me and have loved them even as you have loved me. (John 17:20–23 UPDATED NIV)

Evangelicals have a phrase we often use to describe the heart of our faith: "a relationship with Jesus." And a *relationship* with Jesus is a very good thing; it is far, far different than having a religion. But Jesus is after more—he wants *union* with us; he wants oneness of being. So, the illustration Jesus used in John 17 was, *"Just as* you are in me and I am in you. May they also be in us . . ."* Our greatest need is union with God. Church unity is a beautiful thing and we need it very much, but as I explained in chapter 14, that is not what Jesus was praying for.

The destiny of the human soul is union with God. The same oneness that Jesus talked about with his Father is our destiny as well. That's what we were made for. Prayer is one of his primary means of doing it, drawing us to himself, getting us to pour out our hearts before him so that we can receive his heart toward us. "Communion with God is the one need of the soul beyond all other need," wrote George MacDonald. "Prayer is the beginning of that communion and some need is the motive of that prayer."[2]

You have a soul. God has a soul too. (Isn't that amazing?)

I will make My dwelling among you, and My soul will not reject you. (Lev. 26:11 NASB)

But I will raise up for Myself a faithful priest who will do according to what is in My heart and in My soul. (1 Sam. 2:35 NASB)

Inviting the soul of God into union with your soul will bring about relief you did not know was possible.

You have a heart. God has a heart too.

The LORD was sorry that He had made man on the earth, and He was grieved in His heart. (Gen. 6:6 NASB)

I have consecrated this temple, which you have built, by putting my Name there forever. My eyes and my heart will always be there. (1 Kings 9:3)

Then I will give you shepherds after my own heart, who will lead you with knowledge and understanding. (Jer. 3:15)

Inviting the heart of God into union with your heart will bring about relief you did not know was possible.

The heart and soul experience tragic assault in this war. The two essential categories needing ministry are wounding and brokenness—as we explore these, you will understand why I draw a distinction between the two. But whatever the damage may be, however it was inflicted, however unreachable it might seem, the essence of healing prayer is always bringing the presence of Jesus into the afflicted places, for we are restored through union with him. I am reemphasizing this because sometimes the technicalities draw us away from the simplicity of this type of prayer; I want to make it readily accessible to you.

We simply invoke His presence, then invite Him into our hearts. He shows us our hearts. In prayer for the healing of memories, we simply ask our Lord to come present to that place where we were so wounded (or perhaps wounded another). Forgiving others, and receiving forgiveness, occurs. In prayer for the healing of the heart from fears, bitterness, etc., we see primal fears as well as lesser ones dealt with immediately: those fears that the sufferer often has not been aware of, never been able to name—they only know that their lives have been seriously restricted and shaped because of them.[3]

Wounds

Our team was praying for an older gentleman who had been experiencing profound, unresolved sadness, which he could not name, nor link to any cause. As they prayed, Jesus brought back a memory from when he was five years old. The boy had grown up without a father, who had disappeared shortly after the mom had become pregnant outside of marriage. One day—when he was five—his mother found him running from room to room throughout their house. "What are you looking for, honey?" she asked. "I'm looking for my daddy." I wept.

The loss of a father—or rejection by your father, abandonment, abuse—these are all wounds to the heart and soul. As are the same sorrows coming through a mother, or the absence of a mother. Or a brother, sister, coach, friend, lover, stranger. Think of wounding as taking an arrow to the heart and soul. It can come in so many ways: shame, guilt, betrayal, violation, neglect. The list is nearly endless, and growing more and more extreme as the world spirals deeper into darkness. Do not diminish the wounds you have received because you have heard far "worse" stories than yours; minimizing the impact of a wound never heals it. Jesus cares about it all.

In the spirit of "there is a way things work," the basic approach for healing prayer typically goes like this:

- inviting the presence of Jesus into the wound specifically
- forgiving the one who wounded
- renouncing the message, the lie, breaking any agreement with it
- inviting the presence and healing love of God there

I touched upon listening prayer before getting to this chapter because it plays such a vital role in inner healing. We look to Jesus to guide us through the process in very intimate ways.

Stasi and I were recently praying with a dear young woman over some difficulties in her life. As we quieted ourselves before Jesus, the first thing we prayed was, "Let there be light—shine your light over Tami's life, Lord." We lingered for a moment there; you don't want to rush this kind of prayer, even if you think you know what needs to happen next. Let Jesus lead. I heard the word *contempt*. Now, rather than making conjectures about what *I* thought that might mean, I always try and ask the person we are praying for what *she* thinks it means—for she often knows immediately why Jesus spoke what he did. Tami said, "Oh yes, I remember the day . . ." and we were off and running.

Jesus took us to a pivotal moment from her adolescence, where she had experienced major contempt from an older sister. As so often happens in young girls, it had to do with body issues;

shame and contempt poured out through piercing words and laughter from a jealous sister. That was the wound. We invited the presence of Jesus into this place in her heart and soul. He asked Tami to forgive her sister. This is another moment you don't want to rush through; sometimes it takes time for a person to be ready to forgive. It often helps to explain that forgiveness is not saying it didn't matter; it is not saying we simply choose to overlook the offense. Forgiveness is saying the cross is enough—we require no further payment than Jesus paid. Forgiveness is releasing the person to God for him to deal with.

Tami did, and we were able to press deeper then into healing. Often the enemy will be there, in those wounded or broken places; demons smell human suffering like sharks smell blood in the water, and they will take advantage of the weakness until they are commanded to leave. Tami needed to break agreements with the contempt, as in, "I renounce every agreement I made with this contempt; I renounce the lie that I am worthy of contempt." Then, through our authority in Christ we banished the enemy: "In the name and authority of Jesus Christ we command the foul spirits here to leave now; we bring the mighty victory of Jesus Christ against you, and we send you to your judgment in Jesus' name. All contempt, and every foul spirit, must leave now and never return, in Jesus' name."

Each of these steps clears the way toward the goal—the healing of the wound. Having banished the enemy, we then invited the healing love of Jesus to come to Tami and minister to her. Sometimes the recipient will see Jesus come to him; sometimes he will hear him speak healing words; other times he will simply feel better, feel the love and comfort of God come into his soul. This was the case with Tami; it wasn't dramatic, but beautifully simple. She felt better, and she has continued to feel better to this day.

In cases where the wounding was particularly violent or defiling, we will often add to these steps a time of praying the cleansing blood of Jesus through the wound, through this place in heart and soul. Banishing the enemy is essential here as well, and might require some thorough "house cleaning." We will then ask Jesus to "restore the soul" here (which he does literally, not just figuratively).

Brokenness

I've been in hundreds of counseling and/or healing prayer sessions when the person relating a story suddenly looks the age that she was at the time of the event she is relating. I'll often pause and ask, "How old do you feel right now, as you tell us this story?" And almost invariably, she will hesitate with the newness of the question—the idea never occurred to her before—and then say, "I feel eight," or sixteen or three or what have you.

You can probably relate to what I am describing. Certain places make you feel like a child again when you return there— your childhood home or bedroom, a grade school, the location of a long-forgotten family vacation. Perhaps you have also had the experience of suddenly feeling very young inside when a certain trigger happens—a song or sound, even smells; someone gets angry with you, or touches you, or betrays you as an adult. Perhaps there are memories in which you feel like you are still six years old, or whatever age it was while you were there. However we encounter it, often it does feel as though there are young places within us.

And there are.

One of my favorite passages in all the Bible is the Old Testament passage Jesus quoted in Luke 4 when he announced the beginning of his ministry:

> The Spirit of the Sovereign LORD is on me,
>> because the LORD has anointed me
>> to proclaim good news to the poor.
>
> He has sent me to bind up the brokenhearted,
>> to proclaim freedom for the captives
>> and release from darkness for the prisoners,
>
> to proclaim the year of the LORD's favor
>> and the day of vengeance of our God,
>
> to comfort all who mourn,
>> and provide for those who grieve in Zion—
>
> to bestow on them a crown of beauty
>> instead of ashes,
>
> the oil of joy
>> instead of mourning,
>
> and a garment of praise
>> instead of a spirit of despair. (Isa. 61:1–3 UPDATED NIV)

How beautiful, how hopeful and encouraging that Jesus names this as his most central purpose for our lives! Could anything bring more hope than this? (You must remember that *salvation* as understood in both the Old and New Testaments means a total rescue of the human being; yes, rescue from the terrors of hell, but also the wholeness of life and being that God brings through re-creation and restoration.)

The word *brokenhearted* as used by Isaiah (and by Jesus, by way of highlighting the passage) is not just a metaphor for sadness or grief. Isaiah used the Hebrew word *shabar* elsewhere in his writing to describe actual breaking—such as what happens when a statue falls to the ground and shatters, or when dry branches are broken into pieces to be used in the fire. He is talking about a *literal* breaking of the heart (referring to our "inner" hearts, the heart Jesus talked about often, not our physical hearts).

Psychologists will sometimes refer to this as "arrested development," when part of our inner being becomes "stuck" at a certain age. It is also called fragmentation, or DID—Dissociative Identity Disorder—an attempt to describe the inner being in need of reintegration. However you choose to describe it, the reality we have seen perhaps a thousand times now in our ministry is that most of us have younger places within us that need the healing ministry of Jesus. A wound does not necessarily result in this brokenness, this fragmentation; wounds do pierce us, painfully, but some events actually shatter part of our inner beings and that broken part remains at the age when the event took place. This is usually true in cases of sexual abuse, but it extends far beyond abuse.

As we learn to walk with God and recognize his voice, he is able to raise this deeper brokenness to the surface. The process for healing from brokenness is very much like it is for wounds, with a few additional and important differences because we are talking about fragmentation, or separation from ourselves; we are addressing actual brokenness within.

> Teach me your way, O LORD,
> and I will walk in your truth;

give me an undivided heart,
> that I may fear your name.
I will praise you, O Lord my God, with all my heart;
> I will glorify your name forever. (Ps. 86:11–12)

The "undivided heart" is what we are after. As with healing prayer for woundedness, we begin by inviting Jesus in. We ask him to shine his light into the broken places he is trying to reach. Sometimes he will take us back to a memory, a time and place when a shattering blow was given. Sometimes he will simply make us aware of a "young" place in our hearts, a younger "us" that needs his love and comfort. Pay attention. Keep inviting Christ in.

We ask Jesus what he is saying to this broken place within us. Jesus will often speak words of love or comfort to this specific young part of our hearts. Sometimes he will ask us a question, like, *Why are you sad?* or *Why are you frightened?* Often he will ask, *Will you let me come to you?* Remember, he says he stands at the door and knocks, waiting for us to open the door for him to come in (Rev. 3:20). He waits for our permission to come and heal. Quite often these broken places "hide" behind the older parts of our personalities, and that is why Jesus lovingly and gently invites them to come forward by asking questions.

What we are praying toward in these cases of actual brokenness is *integration*—we want to be made whole again. "Give me an undivided heart," as David prayed. As we invite Jesus to come and bind up our broken hearts, sometimes he will ask us to take his hand and he will lead us out from the memory, out from hiding. Often we simply feel his love and presence there in ways we have never felt before. As with wounding, it often includes forgiving the ones who hurt us and releasing them to Jesus.

Self-rejection plays a major role here. It is quite common for the older part of us to feel embarrassment, or anger, or shame about the younger "stuck" place. And therefore common for us to express rejection toward this part of us. We push it away, push it to the background. That is why it is important for us to renounce all self-rejection also, for Jesus cannot integrate us while we are rejecting these places within us.

As we linger in prayer, we ask Jesus to come and find the broken place(s) and bring them into the safety of his love. When Isaiah described this healing ministry of Jesus, the prophet linked integration with deliverance: "He has sent me to bind up the brokenhearted, to proclaim freedom for the captives and release from darkness for the prisoners" (Isa. 61:1).

I mentioned above that the enemy will often use places of wounding as occasions to oppress us; the same holds true for brokenness. In fact, it is more common to find spiritual warfare in broken places because the chasm in the heart and soul provides a place for the enemy to do his work. He is a divider, after all; his main work is to divide—man from God, man from one another, and man from himself. So as we seek integration, we ask Jesus to bring his sword against the enemies that are "holding back" the young places, or oppressing them in some way.

We then ask Jesus for *integration*—to restore us in wholeheartedness, to heal up the brokenness and make us whole again, through his presence within us. We ask him to bring the young place into that wonderful home Jesus has made for himself in our hearts (Eph. 3:17). The young parts of us feel safe with Jesus there; it is a place filled with love. And in that place Jesus can bring healing about, either in a moment or sometimes over time.

Becoming Whole Is a Process

"Healing prayer," said Leanne Payne, "is not the 'instant fix,' nor the bypassing of slow and steady growth. It is that which clears the path and makes such progress possible."[4] This type of prayer is beautiful and indispensable in our journey toward maturity, toward holiness, toward wholeness. But the journey requires other things as well—often counseling, certainly discipleship, and, to borrow Eugene Peterson's phrase, "a long obedience in the same direction."[5] There is no zap that suddenly makes a person as whole and beautiful as Jesus Christ. Wholeness is something we grow into as we walk with Jesus through the years of our lives. Knowing this actually takes a great deal of pressure off—that pressure to find the instant fix or have the One Defining Moment. It releases us to walk with God and allow him to personalize our healing journey.

For further reading:

Leanne Payne: *The Healing Presence*

Charles Kraft: *Deep Wounds, Deep Healing*

Bethelsozo.com: a very simple and effective inner-healing approach

Sixteen

PHYSICAL HEALING

Is anyone among you sick? Let them call the elders of the church to pray over them and anoint them with oil in the name of the Lord. And the prayer offered in faith will make the sick person well; the Lord will raise them up. (James 5:14–15 UPDATED NIV)

Earlier in this book I used physical healing as an example of how prayer is *partnering* with God because it is such a practical expression of the partnership. We don't pretend it is by our power that healing comes; and yet, God has us "get involved" through the laying on of hands. We do our part; he does his. We do *not* have to conjure the healing; this is so helpful to know and hang on to because trying hard, straining, and stressing actually gets in the way.

Now, there is nothing that helps healing prayer more than having some personal experience of seeing it happen. (Faith does play a role in this.) Nothing overcomes our unbelief like seeing it happen for ourselves; even more so as a result of our own prayers! Therefore, start with small prayer projects. Headaches are a good beginning, or a sore throat. You didn't learn how to read by studying Shakespeare, nor did you learn to drive by starting with freeway on-ramps at sixty-five miles per hour. Don't start your experiments in healing with cancer or broken bones.

The Basics

What we are doing in healing prayer is bringing the body into a place where the power of God can flow into the affliction— *especially* into the places of affliction. We are also presenting ourselves to be used of God as channels of that healing power.

Step One: Consecrate the body and the specific places needing healing.

> Therefore, I urge you, brothers and sisters, in view of God's mercy, to offer your bodies as a living sacrifice, holy and pleasing to God—this is your true and proper worship. (Rom. 12:1 UPDATED NIV)

Consecration, as we have seen, brings the consecrated object back under the rule of Jesus, into his kingdom, and therefore available to his blessing. But before you have the person you are praying for consecrate his body to Jesus, you will benefit from first consecrating yourself! (We typically do this first thing in a session, or before the session if we can.) You are wanting to be used by God to heal; you are offering yourself to be a vessel of his life and power. Therefore, in order to be a better conduit, it is right for you to consecrate your life to Jesus Christ—including your gifting and hearing. The more holy the vessel, the more power can flow through.

> Lord Jesus—we present ourselves to you now to be your partners in prayer, to be your vessels of healing. We consecrate to you our body, soul, and spirit, our heart, mind, and will. We consecrate to you our gifting, our hearing, all our prayers. Cleanse us with your blood, Lord; restore us and renew us. Holy Spirit, fill us afresh; restore our union with Jesus, and restore the power of Jesus in us; we ask you to guide and fill this time of prayer.

Then invite the person being prayed for to consecrate her body to God. It is important to have the person being prayed for do this (unless of course she is unconscious, or in the case of a sleeping child). After all, it is *her* body; she has authority over it—and the kingdom works on the basis of authority. Be as specific as you can. General and unspecific prayers typically see general and unspecific results.

> Lord Jesus, I present my body to you now as a living sacrifice. I consecrate all the faculties of my body to Jesus Christ and to him alone. I consecrate [the specific part of the body needing healing]. I bring my body fully under your rule and under your dominion. My body belongs to you, Lord, and I consecrate it to you right now fully, totally, completely.

We have found it often helps to renounce any misuse of the body, for typically it is those abuses that have made the body subject to affliction (and of course sin is what gives the enemy a claim on us as well). For example, you are praying for the healing of ulcers. You want to ask, "Where did the ulcers come from?" Was it alcohol abuse? Anger and rage? You will find healing prayer a difficult thing to accomplish until the person repents of those things; they were the open door to the suffering.

Oftentimes in acts of consecration, repentance is required. This isn't always necessary, but you will find it helpful if your first pass at prayer does not begin to produce results. For example,

Jesus, I renounce every misuse of my body, and I renounce all forms of sin through my body or against my body. I renounce [whatever it may have been—drug abuse, overeating, binging and purging, anger, rage, etc.]. By the blood of Jesus Christ I now cancel every claim I have given the enemy against my body. I cancel every form of access or dominion my actions have given the enemy against my body, through the cross and blood of the Lord Jesus Christ, and I rededicate my body as a temple of the living God, a vessel of his holy life.

Step Two: Invoke the life of God.

The mechanics of healing prayer are quite simple: we are invoking the life force of God into the afflicted body to restore it. This is the power that raised Jesus from the dead, the power that gives life to and sustains all creation. There is plenty of it to go around (four hundred billion billion suns' worth, and more!). So as we begin to invoke the healing power of God, we will often pray scriptures that help us open ourselves to it, and call it into the *specific* places of suffering:

> O God, you are our life. You are Nancy's life. You have
> breathed into us the breath of life, and we have become living
> beings (Gen. 2:7). Our very existence and our being flow
> from you. In you we live and move and have our being (Acts
> 17:28). Jesus—you are the Vine, and we are true branches of
> yours (John 15:5). Nancy is a true branch of yours. Father,
> you have made Nancy alive with Christ (Eph. 2:4–5). Dear
> Father, we give Nancy to you now to be filled with your life.
> Restore this frail branch in full union with Jesus who is the
> Vine. Restore her full union with Christ and with you. We
> call forth the mighty life of Jesus Christ to flow into Nancy
> now. May your life and resurrection power flow now into her
> body, and into these afflicted places. [Be specific—call the
> life of God into the places of pain and brokenness.] You are
> the God who gives life to the dead (Rom. 4:17). And if the
> Spirit of him who raised Jesus from the dead is living in us
> (and you are living in us), he who raised Jesus from the dead
> will also give life to our mortal bodies through his Spirit,
> who lives in me (Rom. 8:11). Mighty Spirit of God, we call
> forth your power into this body, and into every place of
> affliction. O God, fill Nancy with the resurrection power of
> Jesus Christ.

This is just a model, a type of approach. As you follow the Holy Spirit, he will lead you. But remember: *you are not striving*! No amount of anguish or trying hard will increase the amount of life that is flowing through you. In fact, all forms of striving close off the channels of your life to be a vessel of his life. Relax. Settle into it.

Use the authority of Jesus Christ given to you. In many of the cases where we see Jesus performing a healing, he actually doesn't touch the person—he simply commands it!

> We declare and we enforce the authority of Jesus Christ over Nancy and over her body. We bring the authority of Jesus Christ over her body and over these afflicted places [be specific]. By the authority we have in the name of Jesus Christ, we command the restoration of this body; we command the complete restoration of [specific places]. In the authority of Jesus Christ, we call forth the mighty healing power of Jesus into this body . . .

Like that.

The passage in James on healing prayer recommends anointing with oil; Stasi and I try to keep anointing oil with us at all times for this very purpose. If we forgot, we'll raid the cupboards and use whatever oil we find there—olive oil, cooking oil, whatever there is to work with. Anointing is not a law; healing can flow without it. But it is a vessel through which the Lord can work, and it often helps the faith of the person being prayed for, helps them open themselves to the healing presence of God.

Step Three: Give it *time!*

Picture an empty well. You are turning on a hose to fill that well; it is going to take some time. "Wait upon the Lord." Give it time as you pray; don't rush it. (I'm continually surprised how short most Christians' prayers are—like, a minute or two. That barely gets things going; that is not going to accomplish much at all. As noted earlier, it's like trying to fell a tree with one stroke of an axe.) Stay there, laying on hands if need be; stay and linger, and as you do, repeat the prayers of invoking the life of God into the afflicted place. Linger for fifteen, twenty minutes or more. Often we will just linger praying/commanding/invoking *life* . . . *life* . . . *life*.

Worship really helps. Remember—you are looking to Jesus, not to the problem. Turn on some worship music if you can as you begin your session. Worship first, because it rouses the spirit of everyone present to look to Jesus. After we have consecrated and prayed our first round of prayers, we will turn up the worship music for a few songs and just worship "over" the body, still laying on hands, still praying but in worship too.

Proclaiming is also very helpful. Announcing (and therefore enforcing) truth like:

> "Do you not know that your bodies are temples of the Holy Spirit, who is in you, whom you have received from God? You are not your own; you were bought at a price" (1 Cor. 6:19–20 UPDATED NIV). Jesus, we declare and we proclaim that Jason's body is yours and yours alone. He has been bought with a price, with the blood of Christ. Holy Spirit, this is your temple—come and fill your temple now with the healing power of God.
>
> "And if the Spirit of him who raised Jesus from the dead is living in you, he who raised Christ from the dead will also give life to your mortal bodies because of his Spirit who lives in you" (Rom. 8:11 UPDATED NIV). Spirit of God, come and give life to Jason's mortal body by the power of God within him.

Step Four: Watch for the cloud rising from the sea.

It is helpful to have the person you are praying for share with you any changes she is feeling in her body as you pray. This includes positive changes: "Wow—when you guys started worshiping over me, I felt a warmth through my body." In that case, worship more (or whatever produced the change)! But also report any negative changes, "My headache just got worse," because that is immediate data that you are dealing with some sort of stronghold and it will guide your prayers in step five.

Step Five: Address the demonic.

I find it fascinating that in a number of episodes where Jesus brought physical healing to someone, he actually did it by banishing foul spirits: "Then they brought him a demon-possessed man who was blind and mute, and Jesus healed him, so that he could both talk and see" (Matt. 12:22).

The enemy hates us; his human allies such as witches hate us, too, and they curse Christians. So it is very likely that in a number of situations where you are trying to bring physical healing, you will need to break the enemy's work there as well. Sometimes you will pick it up as soon as you begin to pray—you feel the hatred over his life, or you feel the dark spirits trying to push you away and keep you from praying. Listen and ask Christ, "Is something here causing this? Are there foul spirits here?"

In fact, often before I ever begin the prayer session, or as soon as we get started, I will ask Jesus, "*Is this physical, or is this spiritual, Lord?*" I'll linger there, and wait. "*Is this affliction physical, or is this spiritual, Lord?*" My reason for asking is simple: if the affliction is based in spiritual attack, meaning, some sort of demonic assault or witchcraft, then no amount of regular healing prayer will fix it. You have to deal with the warfare, and then you can pray for healing. Now, I'm sure there are exceptions to the rule, but our experience has proven this to be helpful in hundreds of cases.

Then we bring the work of Christ against the assault, as we discussed in chapter 14. It is far more effective when you can be specific; ask Jesus to name the foul spirits involved, so you can kick them out by name.

> We bring the body of Jesus Christ, broken for Nancy, against every foul and unclean spirit here. We bring the blood of Jesus Christ and the power of his cross against every foul and unclean spirit here—against every spirit of [name them—all spirits of affliction, destruction, death, etc.]. You are disarmed by the cross and blood of Jesus Christ; you have been defeated by the power of his resurrection. All authority in the heavens and on the earth has been given to Jesus Christ, and at his name every knee must bow. We bring the authority of Jesus Christ and the mighty victory of Jesus Christ against each and every foul spirit here, and we order you bound and banished to your judgments. You must leave Nancy now, and you must leave her body. Now. We bind and banish you, and we forbid you to transfer or return, in the mighty name of Jesus Christ who is Lord of the heavens, and Lord of the earth.

Another category to be aware of are curses. Ask Jesus if there are curses operating here. Then break their power as we discussed in chapter 14.

We bring Jesus Christ, cursed for Nancy, cursed for each
of us, against every form of curse operating here. "Christ
redeemed us from the curse of the law by becoming a curse
for us, for it is written: 'Cursed is everyone who is hung
on a pole'" (Gal. 3:13 UPDATED NIV). We bring Jesus Christ
cursed against every form of curse, and we break their
powers now and forever, by the mighty name of Jesus Christ
the Lord.

This would include self-cursing (which is actually very common). Recall the story I told earlier, about trying to pray for healing of the man who had recurring illness, and Jesus asked him how he felt about his body, and he said, "I hate my body." He needed to break those agreements and renounce cursing himself to clear the way for healing prayer. If you seem to be encountering resistance bringing the life of God into his body, ask him how he feels about his body. Have him renounce all judgments, hatred, and self-rejection.

Step Six: Curse the illness.

Early in the morning, as Jesus was on his way back to the city,
he was hungry. Seeing a fig tree by the road, he went up to it
but found nothing on it except leaves. Then he said to it, "May
you never bear fruit again!" Immediately the tree withered.
(Matt. 21:18–19 UPDATED NIV)

The Bible takes blessing and cursing very seriously because it is real; it *works*. In both Testaments we see godly men and women respecting the power of blessing, and cursing. Jesus does so. Now, yes—we are told not to curse people. But Christ by example does open the possibility for us to curse physical objects, and we have found it effective in cases of difficult illness and even cancer to curse the illness. It is a thief and destroyer. It is a foul presence in the body. It is an *intruder*! You are banishing it from the body as you pray—you might as well go full-on and curse it directly.

You may or may not feel comfortable doing this, but keep it as an arrow in your quiver for those situations where no breakthrough is coming.

Stay with It!

Physical healing can be immediate. But it can also take time, especially in cases of profound or chronic suffering. I absolutely love this story of Jesus taking more than one pass to heal a man:

> They came to Bethsaida, and some people brought a blind man and begged Jesus to touch him. He took the blind man by the hand and led him outside the village. When he had spit on the man's eyes and put his hands on him, Jesus asked, "Do you see anything?"
>
> He looked up and said, "I see people; they look like trees walking around."
>
> Once more Jesus put his hands on the man's eyes. Then his eyes were opened, his sight was restored, and he saw everything clearly. (Mark 8:22–25)

Whatever you want to make of this wild story, you have to admit it took Christ more than one pass to fully heal the man.

Surely this was for our benefit, another way of encouraging us to pray and not give up!

For further reading:

Agnes Sanford: *The Healing Light*

Bill Johnson and Randy Clark: *The Essential Guide to Healing*

Seventeen

HOLDING THE HEART
IN EVERY OUTCOME

Several months ago Stasi and I traveled to Hawaii to visit friends and finish this book. But honestly, I see now we were hoping to re-create a moment in time. Two years before we had gone to see our friends and drink deeply from the springs of rest and restoration that seem to flow so easily in the islands. During that idyll we had what remains one of those days—the days you look back on and say, "That was one of the best days of our lives." A postcard-perfect day with the ocean so unbelievably clear and azure; the clouds those pastel puffs you only see in the tropics; the trade winds soft and warm on our skin. Our friends took us out on their little sailing canoe to enjoy the ocean and look for dolphins and whales.

Being on the ocean in a small, lithe craft on a beautiful, sunny morning is like floating on the joy of God—the incomprehensible power and depth, the whimsy and majesty, the vast, playful beauty in every direction.

The day became enchanting. More than spotting the dolphins and whales, we got to *swim* with them. First it was the lively spinner dolphins, in a pod of about fifty or sixty, headed on a course straight for our boat. We donned snorkel gear and jumped in, waiting with held breath for their approach. They came right under us, around us—playful, curious, darting in and out so bright and intelligent, but then darting just as easily away, indifferent in their secretive joy, like elves of the sea.

Later we found the whales—humpbacks the size of small submarines. As we dove back in the water (we are in the open ocean, mind you), we could hear them calling to one another, musical, haunting, first high notes, followed by notes so deep they resounded in your chest, echoing off into the deep. Then there was lying in the sun warming ourselves, the lazy day on the water, the easy conversation, the feast afterward. As I fell asleep to the sound of breakers that night, I could hear the cries of the whales echoing in my soul.

It was simply glorious, one of those once-in-a-lifetime experiences you hope isn't once in a lifetime.

That was two years ago. We came back, as I said, to visit our friends, and hopefully finish up this book. But we forgot one of the deep truths of this life: you can rarely hit the "repeat" button. The day we arrived a rainstorm was passing through the islands. Day two the wind kicked up to almost gale proportions, clearing the beaches and pinning all boats in the harbor; paradise was not paradisiacal. (It was incessant, strong winds on open prairies that drove previous generations mad.) On top of that we faced serious warfare there; we spent much of our time shutting it down through prayer.

Our hopes were deferred, and as Scripture says, "Hope deferred makes the heart sick" (Prov. 13:12).

Yes, it was gorgeous. The tropical sun came out; the ocean was still glorious; the flowers as exotic as they've always been. But we did have to let go our secret expectations. We had to recalibrate. The trip had lovely moments, but it was nothing like we'd hoped.

And we prayed hard over that trip. So did our friends.

What Are We to Do?

Now, I was very aware while I sat there in the stormy islands that our dear friend was still lying in a hospital bed in Houston, his battle with cancer taking a terrible toll—not only on his body, soul, and spirit, but on his spouse, family, and friends. I was very aware that the daughter of other friends was still on the streets, breaking her parents' hearts. A young man we care about was still in a state of mental illness; our sweet adopted daughter faced another year alone. I was very, *very* aware of the unanswered prayers all around us. These are the moments we must "guard our hearts," as Scripture urges:

> Above all else, guard your heart,
>> for it is the wellspring of life. (Prov. 4:23)

Never was this more urgently needed than in the cases of unanswered prayer. We tried it; we went out on a limb; we put our hopes in God. Now what are we to do? It can feel like free-falling into the abyss. How do we guard our hearts, and our faith? I think I can help you with that; I think I can help you not give way to defeat or despair.

First—be *very* careful how you interpret "unanswered prayer." Our hearts are so vulnerable in these moments. It's just too easy to lose heart. The conclusions come rushing in—*God isn't listening; he doesn't care; I'm not faithful enough; prayer doesn't really work.* Catch yourself! Don't let your heart go there! Ask Jesus to help you interpret what is going on. *Jesus—catch my heart,* is the first thing I always pray. *Catch my heart, Lord. Help me interpret what is going on here.* Beware those nasty, soul-killing agreements.

The disappointment is real. I appreciate that the scripture admits deferred hope makes the heart sick because that sure is true in my experience; it assures me that God knows it does too. He said so. The disappointment of unanswered prayer can be devastating. We need to invite the love of God into the disappointment; we need his ministry there. We may need to shed some tears; we may need to grieve; we might need to take a baseball bat to a trash can. However we express our heartsickness, we *must* invite Jesus there—just like we do with inner healing prayer—to comfort, heal, and restore.

I have had to add another phrase to my journal on who God is, and who I am:

God is not a betrayer—he does not betray and he has never betrayed me.

Because unanswered prayer that was urgent and beyond precious to you can feel like a knife to the heart. The enemy rushes in with feelings of betrayal; he whispers terrible things about God in our vulnerability. It is never, ever true. But sometimes I have to remind myself of that.

Should we resolve ourselves to stick it out and not give up? Honestly . . . it depends. Yes, we have Elijah's resolve on the mountain, and his perseverance with no evidence that things were working until right at the end, after the eighth round. We have Daniel, and the long silence of God before he had any interpretation for it. We watched the church at Mary's house going at it all night, strenuously, to free Peter. We will probably have to stick at it long past what we thought we would.

But like any other form of total-life exertion, we do need periods of rest. Even God rested, on the seventh day. It often helps our hearts—and our prayers—to give a long prayer vigil a rest now and then. This is part of the beauty of listening prayer, this ability to ask Jesus and flow with him through all the ins and outs of prayer. After a rest you will find yourself in a much better place to go at it again, and you may receive new guidance that enables you to adjust your prayers in a more effective direction.

Having said that—having said the previous sixteen chapters—I also need to say that there is a time to let it go.

I do *not* mean you let your faith in the goodness of God go.

I do *not* mean you let praying go.

But there is a time to let contending go, let go the Prayer of Intervention when you have done all you can and more. As you stay close to Jesus, he will let you know when that time is.

Friends, we are maturing. I need to call upon that maturity now, to hold two things that seem opposite before you. Massive amounts of healing, restoration, goodness, and beauty are available to us as we take mature prayer seriously. But not every prayer will bring the outcome you want, and what will you do with that? I think we need to put all of this within a higher and greater context; I believe that will help us, profoundly.

The Partial

"A sower went out to sow some seed . . ." So begins one of the most famous of the story-lessons Jesus left recorded for us. You recall how it goes: Some of that precious seed gets eaten by birds, some sprouts but withers quickly, and some is strangled by those infamous weeds. Only one in four makes it to good soil. A famous metaphor, but I think we've missed one of the staggering implications.

Less than half the seeds that Jesus plants ever bear the fruit he longs for.

The Son of God is the sower; he says so himself. He then honestly admits that even *his* efforts prevail only some of the time. Not all of the time—some of the time. One in four. Jesus implies that his batting average is about .250. And this is *Jesus* we are talking about—the man who walked on water, calmed the storm, fed five thousand, raised Lazarus and a few other people from the dead. What do you make of that?

You are going to have to come to terms with the partial nature of this life. Have you come to terms yet with the partial?

The longing for life is the driving force of all humanity. "We can never give up longing and wishing while we are thoroughly alive," wrote George Eliot. "There are certain things we feel to be beautiful and good, and we *must* hunger for them."[1] It is our longing for life that compels us to pray; the same desire sustains us through long and difficult prayer. When we see what is possible as the kingdom of God invades this world, hope surges within us and that is *good*.

What is not good is the subtle shift that sometimes follows. When our hearts get a taste of the life we were meant for, desire awakens within us like a grizzly bear who caught the scent of something it likes on the wind. When life begins to come together in a way we have always longed it would, something deep inside us whispers, *Maybe it can always be like this.* Maybe we can go back to Hawaii. It is the longing for Eden rising within us, and it is beautiful and powerful. Only . . . it is premature.

Paul saw some pretty staggering answers to prayer as he fought for the beachhead that was early Christianity. He healed people; he cast out demons; he brought salvation to thousands; he raised the dead. But he was also stoned and left for dead; he was shipwrecked three times; five times he received the "thirty-nine lashes" (once was supposed to kill a man); he faced many sleepless nights; he knew exposure, hunger, and cold. And remember—*all of heaven was committed to this man being successful.* His life was magnificent, powerful, triumphant. But no, Paul did not try and make his life like retirement in Hawaii. He knew there is only one paradise—and we are not there yet.

Have you reconciled yourself to the partial?

Are you able to hold on to your faith when only some prayers are answered?

It takes genuine maturity.

Most people don't even try to learn the ways of the kingdom; they just go about their days with a practical agnosticism, hoping things work out, tossing up prayers like they hope to score on a Jesus lottery ticket. They have little to show for it. Others discover the possibility of breakthrough for sons and daughters, allies of God; they begin to experience breathtaking results. Then their Eden-heart gets confused about what it means to be victorious.

We can always be victorious—it just depends on what you

mean by victorious. Or better, it depends on what God means by victorious.

What Is the Goal of This Life?

When I was a boy in the grade-school years, come the end of summer I would actually look forward to the beginning of the new term. It was a chance to reconnect with friends and swap stories of our adventures; we had new shirts and shorts, new lunch boxes; and many a new crush was formed with the cute girls in their summer-rich tans. Besides, for the first few days at least, our teachers took it slow and school seemed a lark, a happy reunion. For the first few days. Then the real class work began, and we all realized this wasn't merely an extension of summer; vacation was over and it was time to learn and grow and apply ourselves.

Dear ones, our real class work has just begun. God is growing us all up. The goal of that maturity—much to our surprise—is not a life free from affliction. Not yet. There is something even greater than happiness, something far higher he has for us.

Last summer Stasi sat with our dear friend as he lay in the hospital, torn by a series of fevers and chills no one could explain. The intense pain dragged on from weeks to months; his large body shrunk from weight loss. Exhaustion—that deep exhaustion brought on through chronic pain—had worn his voice down to a whisper. One afternoon as she sat with him, his body kept going in and out of convulsive shivering. Each time the shaking would pause, he could regain some breath and use it to say in a feeble voice, "I love you, Jesus. I worship you. I love you, Jesus. I worship you."

It was one of the holiest things she had ever witnessed.

His wife has shared in the suffering every step of the way, bearing the additional pain that comes from watching someone you love suffer and not being able to do a thing about it. Several months later, after another round in the hospital where it seemed her husband might be dying, vomiting through the night so hard it broke blood vessels all through his face and still the doctors could not administer treatment, she sent us this:

> I had this beautiful picture of us in the Throne Room, right at the feet of the Father in the Holy of Holies, with oil dripping, then pouring down on us—your prayers ministering to us both. This hospital room WAS the Holy of Holies. I am holding on to that picture and feeling honored God chose us for this fight, to be by his side in this excruciating, yet hidden and holy place. I am overwhelmed by God's provision—yes, He gives us what we need, it is right here—His love, strength and commitment to minister and bring us into the fullness of life no matter where or what is going on.

These people have been through absolute hell, years of it, and this is what they have to say?

I take my shoes off.

I put my hands over my face, as the seraph angels do in the presence of God.

Another lifelong friend of ours, a dear lover of Jesus, was paralyzed in an accident thirty years ago. He has spent the last thirty years of his life—the "prime" of his life—in a wheelchair. Absolutely nothing has been easy. Once a rugged outdoorsman, now getting out of bed and ready for the day takes massive effort.

His body has been hit with all sorts of afflictions that accompany paralysis—immune deficiencies, various infections, and the intense pain that comes with it. On the thirty-year anniversary of his fall he sent me this text:

No regrets.

I am speechless.

The beauty of this holiness is unparalleled by anything else in all creation.

My dear readers—what do you do with the fact that hundreds of thousands of the dearest and most valiant saints would tell you that even though they have passed through terrible affliction, their most precious and fervent prayers unanswered, they would not trade it for anything in the world? They would not trade it because of what they have learned of God, learned of love, learned of hope.

The goal of human existence is union with God, an absolute union of heart, soul, mind, and strength, the union Jesus knew with his Father: "I and the Father are one" (John 10:30). God is weaning us to the place we will be able to say like David, "Your love is better than life" (Ps. 63:3), to truly and actually believe in the marrow of our bones that God's love surpasses anything this world has to offer. To find Jesus Christ as our absolute all-in-all. To be able to say with Paul, "For to me, to live is Christ and to die is gain" (Phil. 1:21). And how did Paul learn that most precious of all lessons? "I consider everything a loss because of the surpassing worth of knowing Christ Jesus my Lord, for whose sake I have lost all things" (Phil. 3:8 UPDATED NIV).

He learned it through loss; he learned it through suffering.

This is what the men and women who speak of God after years of profound suffering have to say. This is the most beautiful form of holiness; God has become everything to them. And dear friends—God is deeply committed to shaping this very holiness in *us*. This is the outcome of the maturity we have been talking about.

> His children are not his real, true sons and daughters until they think like him, feel with him, judge as he judges, are at home with him, and without fear before him because he and they mean the same thing, love the same things, seek the same ends . . .
>
> He will have them share in his being and nature—strong wherein he cares for strength; tender and gracious as he is tender and gracious; angry where and as he is angry. Even in the small matter of power, he will have them able to do whatever his Son Jesus could on the earth.[2]

Yes, our maturity certainly involves doing the things Jesus did. Healing and all. But that maturity *also* involves becoming like him in the transformation of our character. It involves holiness—loving God with all our hearts, souls, minds, and strength. Being willing to suffer the loss of everything for him. Choosing him *in the midst* of suffering. Which is to say, having within us the character of Jesus. And how does God shape our character? We hate the answer, but we know it to be true: affliction.

If you say that God does not intend to use affliction, then what in your mind does he then use? Joy does wonderful things for our souls—it soothes, and strengthens, and heals. But joy does not transform people's characters in the same way affliction does. You do not grow when life is good. Any parent knows this. The child wants ice cream and video games. But the child will grow to be a narcissist if he is allowed nothing but ice cream and video games. The most radiant holiness, the most genuine and glorious love is expressed by those whose lives have known affliction. Jesus best among them.

Our *longing* for life keeps confusing us about the *purpose* of life.

We ache for life to come together as it was meant to be. And it will, friends; it *will*. Very soon. But in the meantime, the purpose of life in this hour is not escaping to Hawaii, or whatever your version of happiness may be. Our "education" in this hour, the goal of our maturing is holiness, the beauty of Jesus Christ formed in us, which is something that requires a great deal of maturity to accept (you see how few accept it). By all that is holy and beautiful—*clearly* the purpose of life is not the removal of all affliction, or would we put ourselves above Jesus?

> During the days of Jesus' life on earth, he offered up prayers and petitions with fervent cries and tears to the one who could save him from death, and he was heard because of his reverent submission. Son though he was, he learned obedience from what he suffered and, once made perfect, he became the source of eternal salvation for all who obey him. (Heb. 5:7–9 UPDATED NIV)

Jesus' life was the life of perfected humanity. He was the best man who ever lived. His life was filled with joy. And it was also a life familiar with suffering. More than that—he learned obedience through what he suffered, was perfected through his suffering. Or as *The Message* translation has it, "he learned trusting-obedience by what he suffered, just as we do. Then, having arrived at the full stature of his maturity . . ."

This is not a discouragement to pray. It is the *higher context* within which we pray. It is a higher end than trying to eliminate all suffering. Oh, yes—we are "more than conquerors through him who loved us" (Rom. 8:37). Yes, we are. Sometimes that overcoming looks like a healing, like freeing Peter, like calling down rain to end a drought, like the men and women

> who shut the mouths of lions, quenched the fury of the flames, and escaped the edge of the sword; whose weakness was turned to strength; and who became powerful in battle and routed foreign armies. Women received back their dead, raised to life again.

And sometimes it looks like others,

> who were tortured, refusing to be released so that they might gain an even better resurrection. Some faced jeers and flogging, and even chains and imprisonment. They were put to death by stoning; they were sawed in two; they were killed by the sword.

Now listen to how the entire conversation on victorious faith is brought to its biblical climax:

> These were all commended for their faith, yet none of them received what had been promised, since God had planned

something better for us so that only together with us would they be made perfect. (Heb. 11:33–40 UPDATED NIV)

All were commended for their faith—the ones who shut the mouths of lions, and the ones who died by the sword. Yes, Peter was freed. But James—who died by the sword—also prevailed. Ultimately, he *won*. Death is never defeat for the Christian; death is mighty victory. (Which is a good thing, by the way, because everyone is going to die, friends; you cannot prevent that in prayer, only delay it a bit!)

None of them received what was promised—because Eden will not be restored on the earth until Jesus returns.

The mighty victory is staying true to God. It is maintaining a mature perspective—where God means everything to you—through glorious breakthrough and in the midst of terrible affliction. If you do not hold fast to this, you will be shaken when your prayers do not seem to prevail; you will fall prey to feelings of failure or despair. Or, you will be grasping at promises of unending victory, looking down on those who do not see things as you do. You will be forced to ignore the sufferings of Christ, and our honor in sharing in them.

And you will miss the goal of this life, which is not unending breakthrough, but something far more beautiful and everlasting— the beauty of Jesus Christ, which your Father is committed to forming in you: "God knew what he was doing from the very beginning. He decided from the outset to shape the lives of those who love him along the same lines as the life of his Son. The Son stands first in the line of humanity he restored. We see the original and intended shape of our lives there in him" (Rom. 8:29 MSG).

Life Will Win

After the last embers of the Waldo Canyon Fire finally died out, later that fall, I would walk up in the hills behind our house, surveying the devastation and assessing the coming danger of the inevitable mudslides, now that the land was stripped bare. Even rocks were broken open from the furnace-heat of the fire. When I returned from wandering in a dead world, my shoes and socks were black with ash. I stopped taking those walks after a while; I had had enough with death and destruction. The rains did come, and the mudslides. But then something else came too.

It was the following summer when I returned to the hills, reluctantly. It seemed way too much to hope that summer might bring with it a different message. When I crested the slope above our house, I was literally stopped in my tracks by what I saw. Wildflowers were blooming here, there, *everywhere*—happy little lavender asters, absurdly tall and joyful sunflowers, blood-red Indian paintbrush, clusters of purple penstemon. In greater abundance than I had ever seen before. The deep-rooted yuccas had survived and were shooting up with vigor, as was all the scrub oak. The wild grasses had grown waist high, swaying like a green sea in the light breezes. Someone had washed the land with so much color and life it looked like a Van Gogh painting.

We have staked it all on this—that life wins. Oh, dear friends—*life wins.*

Life wins. Sometimes now, especially if we will pray. But life wins fully, and very soon.

Just as we must fix our eyes on Jesus when we pray, we must also fix our hearts on this one undeniable truth: life will win.

When you know that unending joy is about to be yours, you live with such an unshakable confidence it will almost be a swagger. You can pray boldly, without fear, knowing that, "If this doesn't work now, it will work totally and completely very soon." We can have that kingdom attitude of Daniel's friends, who said, "God is able to deliver, and he will deliver. But if not . . ." we will not lose heart. Period.

In Closing

Which brings us to two simple prayers by which to end our lessons, two prayers we can all enter into, put our collective shoulders to. The first comes at the end of the Bible—this is the last recorded prayer in Scripture, the prayer the church is praying right before Jesus returns: "He who is the faithful witness to all these things says, 'Yes, I am coming soon!' Amen! Come, Lord Jesus!" (Rev. 22:20 NLT).

We cry out for his return and the restoration of all things. "Come back—Jesus, come back," ought to flow naturally and passionately off your lips every day. (If it doesn't, might it be a sign you are looking to arrange for your life here?) The second prayer makes sense as we pray the first:

> In the last days, God says,
>> I will pour out my Spirit on all people . . .
>> before the coming of the great and glorious day of the
>> Lord.
> And everyone who calls
>> on the name of the Lord will be saved. (Acts 2:17, 20–21)

"Pour out your Spirit, Jesus!" We pray for one last great harvest, like fire fighters rescuing every last life they can from a building about to collapse in flames. I love these prayers because they have nothing to do with my immediate life, my struggles. They call me up into a larger story, lift my eyes to the more important things. It's so refreshing not to always be praying for the crisis before me. We can pray these prayers happily, confidently, *triumphantly*, like the great allies of God we are.

We can pray until that day comes when every prayer will be an immediate incarnation, becoming reality even as we speak it, like creation became reality as God spoke it. For we *are* his sons and daughters, and he is maturing us to love all that he loves, and to do all that he does. To move mountains, and more.

Acknowledgments

With thanks to my daughter-in-law Emilie Eldredge for her fabulous research skills, Curtis and the team at Yates and Yates, and my friends and allies at Thomas Nelson.

Appendices

The Prayers

The "Extended" Daily Prayer (mentioned in chapter 9)

My dear Lord Jesus, I come to you now to be restored in you, renewed in you, to receive your life and love and all the grace and mercy I so desperately need this day. I honor you as my Lord, and I surrender every aspect and dimension of my life to you—my spirit, soul, and body; my heart, mind, and will. I cover myself with your blood—my spirit, soul, and body; my heart, mind, and will. I ask your Holy Spirit to restore me in you, renew me in you, and lead me in this time of prayer. In all that I now pray, I stand in total agreement with your Spirit and with all those praying for me by the Spirit of God, and by the Spirit of God alone.*

---

* Again—if you are the head of a household, you will want to include them by substituting:

In all that I now pray, I include [my wife and/or children, by name]. I bring them under my authority and covering, under your authority and covering. I cover them with your blood—their spirits, souls, and bodies; their hearts, minds, and will. I ask your Holy Spirit to restore them in you, renew them in you, and apply to them all that I now pray, acting as their head. In all that I now pray, I stand in total agreement with

Dearest God—holy and victorious Trinity—you alone are worthy of all my worship, my heart's devotion, all my praise, all my trust, and all the glory of my life. I love you, I worship you, I give myself over to you in my heart's search for life. You alone are Life, and you have become my life. I renounce all other gods, I renounce every idol, and I give to you, God, the place in my heart and in my life that you truly deserve. This is all about you, and not about me. You are the Hero of this story, and I belong to you. I ask your forgiveness for my every sin. I renounce sin. Search me, know me, and reveal to me where you are working in my life, and grant to me the grace of your healing and deliverance, and a deep and true repentance.

Heavenly Father, thank you for loving me and choosing me before you made the world. You are my true Father—my creator, redeemer, sustainer—and the true end of all things, including my life. I love you, I trust you, I worship you. I give myself over to you, Father, to be one with you as Jesus is one with you. Thank you for proving your love for me by sending Jesus. I receive him and all his life and all his work which you ordained for me. Thank you for including me in Christ, forgiving me my sins, granting me his righteousness, making me whole and complete in him. Thank you for making me alive with Christ, raising me with him, seating me with him at your right hand, establishing me in his authority, and anointing me with your love and your kingdom. I receive it all with thanks and give it total claim to my life—my spirit, soul, and body; my heart, mind, and will.

I now bring the life and the work of Jesus Christ over my spirit, soul, and body; my heart, mind, and will; over [my wife and children]; our home, this house, and everything in it; over my work; my vehicles and finances; over all my kingdom and domain.

___

your Spirit and with all those praying for me by the Spirit of God and by the Spirit of God alone.

Jesus, thank you for coming to ransom me with your own life. I love you, I worship you, I trust you. I give myself over to you, to be one with you in everything. I receive again all the work and triumph in your cross, blood, and sacrifice for me, through which my every sin is atoned for; I am ransomed and delivered from the kingdom of darkness; transferred to your kingdom; my sin nature is removed and my heart circumcised unto God; and every claim being made against me is canceled and disarmed. I give myself to you again in your cross and death, dying with you to sin, to my flesh, to this world, to the evil one and his kingdom. I take up the cross and crucify my flesh with all its pride, arrogance, unbelief, and idolatry [and anything else you are currently struggling with]. I put off the old man.

I now bring the blood and sacrifice over our union and over my life—my spirit, mind, thoughts, imagination, and gifting; my will, warrior, motive, and aim; my understanding, discernment, and perception; over my sexuality and sensitivity; over my heart and soul and body. I bring your blood and sacrifice over [my wife and children—their spirits, souls, and bodies; their hearts, minds, and will]; over this home, this house, and everything in it; over my work; my vehicles and finances; over all my kingdom and domain.

I now bring the cross, death, blood, and sacrifice of the Lord Jesus Christ against Satan, against his kingdom, against every foul and unclean spirit, every foul power and black art, against every witch, cult, and coven, every trafficking spirit,* against this city, and all cities, counties, states, nations, and kingdoms, and against every human being and his spirit, his warfare and household. I bring the cross, death, blood, and sacrifice of the Lord Jesus Christ to the borders of my kingdom and domain, and I stake it there in Jesus' name.

---

* These are not demons, but the human spirits of the witches that often "travel" to human beings to torment them.

Jesus, I also sincerely receive you as my Life, and I receive all
the work and triumph in your resurrection, through which you have
conquered sin, death, judgment, and the evil one. Death has no power
over you, nor does any foul thing. And I have been raised with you to
a new life, to live your life—dead to sin and alive to God. I take my
place now in your resurrection and in your life, and I give my life to
you to live your life. I am saved by your life. I reign in life through
your life. I receive your hope, love, joy, and faith; your beauty,
goodness, and trueness; your wisdom, power, and strength; your
holiness and integrity in all things.

I now bring the life, resurrection, and empty tomb over our union
and over my life—my spirit, mind, thoughts, imagination, and gifting;
my will, warrior, motive, and aim; my understanding, discernment,
and perception; over my sexuality and sensitivity; over my heart and
soul and body. I bring your life, resurrection, and empty tomb over
[my wife and children—their spirits, souls, and bodies; their hearts,
minds, and will]; over this home, this house, and everything in it; over
my work; my vehicles and finances; over all my kingdom and domain.

I now bring the life, resurrection, and empty tomb of the Lord
Jesus Christ against Satan, against his kingdom, against every foul
and unclean spirit, every foul power and black art, against every
witch, cult, and coven, every trafficking spirit, against this city, and
all cities, counties, states, nations, and kingdoms, and against every
human being and his spirit, his warfare and household. I bring the life,
resurrection, and empty tomb of the Lord Jesus Christ to the borders
of my kingdom and domain, and I stake it there in Jesus' name.

Jesus, I also sincerely receive you as my authority, rule, and
dominion, my everlasting victory against Satan and his kingdom,
and my ability to bring your kingdom at all times and in every way.
I receive all the work and triumph in your ascension, through which

Satan has been judged and cast down, and all authority in heaven and on earth has been given to you. All authority in the heaven realms and all authority on this earth has been given to you, Jesus—and you are worthy to receive all glory and honor, power and dominion, now and forever. I take my place now in your authority and in your throne, through which I have been raised with you to the right hand of the Father and established in your authority. I give myself to you, to reign with you always.

I call down your glory and dominion over union and over my life—my spirit, mind, thoughts, imagination, and gifting; my will, warrior, motive, and aim; my understanding, discernment, and perception; over my sexuality and sensitivity; over my heart and soul and body. I call down glory and dominion over [my wife and children—their spirits, souls, and bodies; their hearts, minds, and will]; over this home, this house, and everything in it; over my work; over my vehicles and finances; over all my kingdom and domain.

I now bring the authority, rule, and dominion of the Lord Jesus Christ, and the full work of Christ, against Satan, against his kingdom, against every foul and unclean spirit—every ruler, power authority, and spiritual force of wickedness, every backup and replacement, every weapon claim and device. [I will name them very specifically now, all I know has been attacking me and all I sense by the Holy Spirit is staged against me this day . . .]. I order them gagged and bound to the judgment of Jesus Christ for them, their backups and replacements, every weapon, claim, and device—by the authority of the Lord Jesus Christ and in his name. I call down the judgment of the Lord Jesus Christ upon the heads of those that refuse to obey, and I send them to their judgment, by the authority of the Lord Jesus Christ and in his name.

I now bring the blood, death, and sacrifice of the Lord Jesus

Christ; I call down the judgment of Christ against every foul power, witchcraft and black art—every hex, vex, and incantation; every spell, veil, shroud, and snare; every ritual sacrifice, implements, dedications, and devices; against every Satanic ritual, their sacrifices, implements, dedications, and devices; against every vow, dedication, and sacrifice; every word, judgment, and curse—written, spoken, unspoken, or transferred to me. I order them disarmed and broken by the authority of the Lord Jesus Christ and in his name.

I now bring the authority, rule, and dominion of the Lord Jesus Christ, and the fullness of the work of Christ against every witch, cult, and coven, every channel and practitioner of black arts. I send the glory of the Lord to them to cut them off and turn them in Jesus' name. I order the trafficking spirit to the throne of Jesus Christ to receive revelation, discipline, and judgment, and then bound to those judgments by the authority of the Lord Jesus Christ and in his name.

I bring the kingdom of God throughout my kingdom and domain against this city, and all cities, counties, states, nations, and kingdoms.

I now bring the authority, rule, and dominion of the Lord Jesus Christ, and the fullness of the work of Christ between me and every human being—his spirit, soul, and body; his sin, warfare, corruption, and projection [extended family members, people I have been counseling, etc.]. I command their human spirits bound back to their bodies, and their sin, warfare, corruption, and projection bound to the work of Christ in their lives. I allow only the love of Christ and the kingdom of God between me and every human being, in Jesus' name.

Holy Spirit, thank you for coming. I love you, I worship you, I trust you. I honor you as Lord of my home, family, kingdom, and domain. I receive all the work and triumph in Pentecost, through which you have come; you have clothed me with power from on high; sealed me in Christ; become my union with the Father and the Son; the

Spirit of truth in me, the life of God in me; my counselor, comforter, strength, and guide. I honor you as Lord, and I fully give to you every aspect and dimension of my spirit, soul, and body; my heart, mind, and will—to be filled with you, to walk in step with you in all things. Fill me afresh, Holy Spirit. Restore my union with the Father and the Son. Lead me into all truth, anoint me for all of my life and walk and calling, and lead me deeper into Jesus today. I receive you with thanks, and I give you total claim to my life.

Heavenly Father, thank you for granting to me every spiritual blessing in Christ Jesus. I claim the riches in Christ Jesus over my life today [my wife and children]. Thank you for your armor; I put on the belt of truth, breastplate of righteousness, shoes of the gospel, helmet of salvation; I take up the shield of faith and sword of the Spirit, and I choose to be strong in the Lord and in the strength of your might, to pray at all times in the Spirit.

Jesus, thank you for your angels. I summon them in the name of Jesus Christ and with love and blessing I instruct them to carry out these orders, to destroy all that is raised against me, to establish your kingdom throughout my home, vehicles, work; to rebuild the shields of protection; and to minister to us your ministry.* I ask you to send forth your Spirit to raise up the full canopy of prayer and intercession for us. I now call forth the kingdom of God throughout my home, my household, my kingdom and domain, in the authority of the Lord Jesus Christ, giving all glory and honor and thanks to him. In Jesus' name, amen.

---

* Hebrews 1:14: "Are not all angels ministering spirits sent to serve those who will inherit salvation?"

A Prayer for Sexual Healing

Your sexuality is deep and core to your nature as a human being. Sexual brokenness can therefore be one of the deepest types of brokenness a person may experience. You must take your healing and restoration seriously. Healing for your sexuality is available! This prayer will help immensely. (You may find you need to pray through it a few times in order to experience a lasting freedom.)

Jesus, I confess here and now that you are my Creator and therefore the creator of my sexuality. I confess that you are also my Savior, that you have ransomed me with your blood and you are therefore the savior of my sexuality. I have been bought with the blood of Jesus Christ; my life and my body belong to God; my sexuality belongs to God. Jesus, I present myself to you now to be made whole and holy in every way, including in my sexuality. You ask us to present our bodies to you as living sacrifices and the parts of our bodies as instruments of righteousness. I do this now. I present my body, my sexuality ["as a man" or "as a woman"] and I present my sexual nature to you.

Lord Jesus Christ, I confess here and now that you are my Creator (John 1:3) and therefore the creator of my sexuality. I confess that you are also my Savior, that you have ransomed me with your blood (Matt. 20:28; 1 Cor. 15:3). I have been bought with the blood of Jesus Christ; my life and my body belong to God (1 Cor. 6:19–20). Jesus, I present myself to you now to be made whole and holy in every way, including in my sexuality. You ask us to present our bodies to you as living sacrifices (Rom. 12:1) and the parts of our bodies as instruments of righteousness (Rom.

6:13). I do this now. I present my body, my sexuality ["as a man" or "as a woman"] and I present my sexual nature to you.

Next you need to renounce the ways you have misused your sexuality. The more specific you can be, the more helpful this will be. Keep in mind there is the "spirit of the law" and the "letter of the law." What matters are issues of heart and mind as well as body. Other examples of sins to renounce would be extramarital affairs, the use of pornography, and sexual fantasies. You may know exactly what you need to confess and renounce; you may need to ask God's help to remember. Take your time here. As memories and events come to mind, confess and renounce them. For example: "Lord Jesus, I ask your forgiveness for my sins of masturbation and using pornography. I renounce those sins in your name." After you have confessed your sins—and don't get tied up trying to remember each and every one, just trust God to remind you—then go on with the rest of the prayer.

Jesus, I ask your Holy Spirit to help me now remember, confess, and renounce my sexual sins. [Pause. Listen. Remember. Confess and renounce.] Lord Jesus, I ask your forgiveness for every act of sexual sin. You promised that if we confess our sins, you are faithful and just to forgive us our sins and cleanse us from all unrighteousness (1 John 1:9). I ask you to cleanse me of my sexual sins now; cleanse my body, soul, and spirit; cleanse my heart and mind and will; cleanse my sexuality. Thank you for forgiving me and cleansing me. I receive your forgiveness and cleansing. I renounce every claim I have given Satan to my life or sexuality through my sexual sins. Those claims are now broken by the cross and blood of Jesus Christ (Col. 2:13–15).

Next comes issues of forgiveness. It is vital that you forgive both yourself and those who have harmed you sexually. *Listen carefully*: Forgiveness is a *choice*; we often have to make the *decision* to forgive long before we *feel* forgiving. We realize this can be difficult, but the freedom you will find will be worth it! Forgiveness is not saying, "It didn't hurt me." Forgiveness is not saying, "It didn't matter." Forgiveness is the act whereby we pardon the person; we release him or her from all bitterness and judgment. We give him or her to God to deal with.

Lord Jesus, I thank you for offering me total and complete forgiveness. I receive that forgiveness now. I choose to forgive myself for all of my sexual wrongdoing. I also choose to forgive those who have harmed me sexually. [Be specific here; name those people and forgive them.] I release them to you. I release all my anger and judgment toward them. Come, Lord Jesus, into the pain they caused me, and heal me with your love.

This next step involves breaking the unhealthy emotional and spiritual bonds formed with other people through sexual sin. One of the reasons the Bible takes sexual sin so seriously is because of the damage it does. Another reason is because of the bonds it forms with people, bonds meant to be formed only between husband and wife (1 Cor. 6:15–20). One of the marvelous effects of the cross of our Lord Jesus Christ is that it breaks these unhealthy bonds. "May I never boast except in the cross of our Lord Jesus

Christ, through which the world has been crucified to me, and I to the world" (Gal. 6:14).

> I now bring the cross of my Lord Jesus Christ between me and
> every person with whom I have been sexually intimate. [Name
> them specifically whenever possible. Also, name those who have
> abused you sexually.] I break all sexual, emotional, and spiritual
> bonds with [name if possible, or just "that girl (or boy) in high
> school" if you can't remember her name]. I keep the cross of
> Christ between us.

Many people experience negative consequences through the misuse of their sexuality. Those consequences might be lingering guilt (even after confession) or repeated sexual temptation. Consequences might also be the inability to enjoy sex with their spouses. It will help to bring the work of Christ here as well. Many people end up making unhealthy "agreements" about sex or themselves, about men or women or intimacy, because of the damage they have experienced through sexual sin (their sin, or the sin of someone against them). You will want to ask Christ what those agreements are, and *break them*!

> I renounce [name what the struggle is—"the inability to have an
> orgasm" or "this lingering shame" or "the hatred of my body"].
> I bring the cross and blood of Jesus Christ against this [guilt or
> shame, every negative consequence]. Lord Jesus, I also ask you
> to reveal to me any agreements I have made about my sexuality
> or this specific struggle. [An example would be "I will always
> struggle with this" or "I don't deserve to enjoy sex now" or "My
> sexuality is dirty." Pause and let Jesus reveal those agreements to

you. Then break them.] I break this agreement [name it] in the name of my Lord Jesus Christ, and I renounce every claim I have given it in my life.

Finally, it will prove helpful to consecrate your sexuality to Jesus Christ once more.

Lord Jesus, I now consecrate my sexuality to you in every way. I consecrate my sexual intimacy with my spouse to you. I ask you to cleanse and heal my sexuality and our sexual intimacy in every way. I ask your healing grace to come and free me from all consequences of sexual sin. I ask you to fill my sexuality with your healing love and goodness. Restore my sexuality in wholeness. Let me and my spouse both experience all of the intimacy and pleasure you intended a man and woman to enjoy in marriage. I pray all of this in the name of Jesus Christ my Lord. Amen!

NOTES

Chapter 1: Prayer That Works

1. *Patch Adams*, directed by Tom Shadyac (Universal City, CA: Universal Pictures, 1998), DVD.

2. Anne Lamott, *Traveling Mercies: Some Thoughts on Faith* (New York: Anchor, 1999), 180.

Chapter 2: Third Graders at Normandy

1. C. S. Lewis, *The Silver Chair* (New York: HarperCollins, 1981), 25.

2. J. R. R. Tolkien, *The Hobbit* (New York: Houghton Mifflin Harcourt, 2012), 190.

3. *The Hobbit: An Unexpected Journey*, directed by Peter Jackson (Leavesden, Hertfordshire: Warner Brothers UK, 2013), DVD.

4. George MacDonald, *Unspoken Sermons* (Whitethorn, CA: Johannesen, 2004), 128.

5. Francis Thompson and Jean Young, *The Hound of Heaven* (Harrisburg, PA: Morehouse, 1992), 24.

Chapter 3: The Cry of the Heart

1. G. K. Chesterton, *The Everlasting Man* (Radford, VA: Wilder, 2008), 118.

2. E. M. Bounds, *E. M. Bounds on Prayer* (Peabody, MA: Hendrickson, 2006), 6, 8.

Chapter 4: Who He Is and Who We Are

1. *The Hobbit: The Battle of the Five Armies*, directed by Peter Jackson (Burbank, CA: Warner Bros. Pictures, 2014), DVD.
2. J. B. Phillips, *Your God Is Too Small* (New York: Simon & Schuster, 2004).
3. T. S. Eliot, *T.S. Eliot-Collected Poems, 1909–1962* (San Diego: Harcourt, Brace & World, 1970), 177.
4. Bette Midler, vocal performance of "From a Distance," arranged by Steve Skinner and Arif Mardin, recorded in 1990, on *From a Distance*, Atlantic, CD.
5. Thomas à Kempis, *The Imitation of Christ* (London: J. M. Dent & Sons, 1960), 61.
6. Thomas à Kempis, *The Imitation Of Christ* (Grand Rapids: Freebook Publisher), n.d., eBook Collection (EBSCOhost), accessed July 14, 2015.
7. Blaise Pascal, *Pensées* (Grand Rapids: Freebook Publisher), n.d., eBook Collection (EBSCOhost), accessed July 14, 2015.

Chapter 5: Bold Authority

1. Nicholas Wolterstorff, *Lament for a Son* (Grand Rapids: Eerdmans, 1987), 19–20.
2. William James, *The Will to Believe: And Other Essays in Popular Philosophy* and *Human Immortality*, reprint edition (Mineola, NY: Courier Corporation, 1956), 61.
3. C. S. Lewis, "The Efficacy of Prayer," *The Atlantic*, vol. 203, no. 1, January 1959, 59–61.
4. C. S. Lewis, *The Horse and His Boy* (New York: HarperCollins, 1982), 209.

Chapter 7: Removing One More Obstacle

1. C. S. Lewis, *The Silver Chair* (New York: HarperCollins, 1981), 24–25.
2. George MacDonald, *Unspoken Sermons* (Whitethorn, CA: Johannesen, 2004), 223.

Chapter 8: Consecration—Bringing Things under the Rule of Jesus

1. Agnes Sanford, *The Healing Light* (New York: Ballentine, 1972), 1.
2. Ibid.

Chapter 9: Daily Prayer

1. Charles M. Guilbert, comp., *The Book of Common Prayer* (New York: Church Hymnal Corporation, 1979), 100.
2. Neil Anderson, *A Way of Escape: Freedom from Sexual Strongholds* (Irvine, CA: Harvest House, 1998), 226.
3. Edward M. Bounds, *The Complete Works of E. M. Bounds on Prayer: Experience the Wonders of God through Prayer* (Grand Rapids: Baker, 2004), 70.

Chapter 10: Pray Now!

1. Thomas Cahill, *How the Irish Saved Civilization: The Untold Story of Ireland's Heroic Role from the Fall of Rome to the Rise of Medieval Europe* (New York: Anchor, Doubleday, 1996), 102.

Chapter 11: "Let There Be Light"—Prayer for Guidance, Understanding, and Revelation

1. J. R. R. Tolkien, *The Two Towers: Being the Second Part of The Lord of the Rings* (Boston: Houghton Mifflin, 1994), 404.

Chapter 12: Listening Prayer

1. Oswald Chambers, *My Utmost for His Highest* (New York: Dodd, Mead and Co., 1963), 124.

Chapter 14: Warfare Prayer

1. William Wordsworth, *Poems, In Two Volumes* (London: Longman, Hurst, Rees, and Orme, 1807), 147.

Chapter 15: Inner Healing—Restoring the Soul

1. Oswald Chambers, *My Utmost for His Highest* (New York: Dodd, Mead and Co., 1963), 219.

2. George MacDonald, *The Heart of George MacDonald: A One-Volume Collection of His Most Important Fiction, Essays, Sermons, Drama, Poetry, Letters,* ed. Rolland Hein (Wheaton, IL: H. Shaw, 1994), 394.

3. Leanne Payne, *The Healing Presence* (Grand Rapids: Baker, 1995), 137.

4. Ibid., 63.

5. Eugene Peterson, *A Long Obedience in the Same Direction: Discipleship in an Instant Society* (Downers Grove, IL: InterVarsity, 2012).

Chapter 17: Holding the Heart in Every Outcome

1. George Eliot, *The Mill on the Floss* (Mineola, NY: Dover, 2003), 244.

2. George MacDonald, *Unspoken Sermons* (Whitethorn, CA: Johannesen, 2004), 283.

ABOUT THE AUTHOR

John Eldredge is the author of numerous bestselling books including *Wild at Heart*, *Fathered by God*, and *Beautiful Outlaw*. He is also director of Ransomed Heart, a ministry devoted to restoring men and women in the love of God. John and Stasi live in Colorado.

RANSOMED HEART'S
FREE GIFT TO YOU

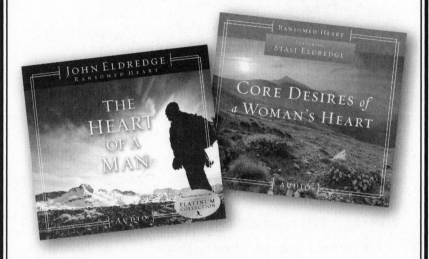

Recorded live, these powerful messages from John and Stasi Eldredge speak to the core desires of the male and female heart. Choose one or both full-length audio downloads.

Visit RansomedHeart.com, click to the Store page, and input the audio title you want (*The Heart of a Man* and/or *Core Desires of a Woman's Heart*). At checkout, type the code HEART and you will receive one or both audio downloads at no charge.

LOVE GOD. LIVE FREE.

JOHN ELDREDGE CLASSICS
With New Content!

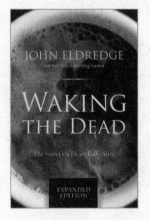

WAKING THE DEAD

This book has been likened to a strong cup of coffee. It will help you see the fierce battle over your heart in this world at war! This edition includes new introductions and "Selah" reflections in every chapter.

WALKING WITH GOD

God offers to speak to us and guide us through each day. To accept that invitation is to enter into an adventure filled with joy and risk, transformation and breakthrough. Now with content on facing the new seasons of life.

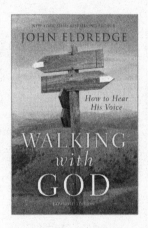

THE JOURNEY OF DESIRE

This book explores the deepest longings of the human heart. If you've been searching for the life you've always dreamed of...this is for you. Features new prayers and reflections in every chapter.

Available wherever books are sold